Match of My Life

FULHAM

Know The Score Books Publications

MATCH OF MY LIFE

FULHAM	Michael Heatley	ISBN 1-905449-51-8
LIVERPOOL	Leo Moynihan	ISBN 1-905449-50-X

CULT HEROES

CHELSEA	Leo Moynihan	ISBN 1-905449-00-3

Match of My Life

FULHAM

Editor: Michael Heatley
Series Editor: Simon Lowe
Know The Score Books Limited

www.knowthescorebooks.com

First published in the United Kingdom
by Know The Score Books Limited, 2005

Know The Score Books Limited
The College Business Centre
Uttoxeter New Road
Derby
DE22 3WZ

www.knowthescorebooks.com

A CIP catalogue record is available for this book from the British Library
ISBN 1-905449-51-8

Jacket and book design by Lisa David

Jacket photography by Thomas Skovsende

Printed and bound in Great Britain
By Cromwell Press, Trowbridge, Wiltshire

Editor's Acknowledgements

Thanks to Dennis Turner, former programme editor of legend, whose name appears on every club history book of note and whose wise counsel is forever appreciated. Likewise Ken Coton, the even more legendary club photographer for so many years, without whose work no Fulham tome would be complete; and publisher Simon Lowe whose idea it was in the first place.

Thanks also go to Paul Warburton of the Fulham Chronicle, Jonathan Lowe, David Lloyd and Debbie and Rebecca at Fulham Football Club for getting behind this book. Your help has been magnificent.

Thumbs-up to Martin Plumb, who put us in touch with Steve Earle, Alex White, and Hammersmith-Enders Drew, Joe, Gavin and Paul.

Finally, a big thank-you to the players we have featured, whose time and co-operation was given in every case without mention of personal reward. We hope we've done you and your memories justice.

Michael Heatley
September 2005

Photographs in this book are reproduced by kind permission of: Action Images, Colorsport, Ken Coton, EMPICS, Fulham Chronicle, Fulham Football Club, Manchester United Football Club & Mirrorpix

Front cover:
Left Alan Mullery shakes the hand of Billy Bonds before the 1975 FA Cup Final
Right Simon Morgan celebrates defeating Premiership leaders Aston Villa in 1999

Rear cover:
Top Where it all began. Rod McAree's winner at Carlisle started Fulham's rise up the divisions back in 1997
Bottom Sean Davis is rather pleased that he has just scored the goal that has won Fulham the First Division title in 2001

Contents

Introduction

The home-spun, olde-worlde virtues of Fulham Football Club have been appreciated by relatively few when measured against a Manchester United or a Liverpool – but those who have enjoyed life by the Thames have included players as well as supporters. Tosh Chamberlain, George Cohen and foreword writer Johnny Haynes were all one-club men, Jim Stannard and Gordon Davies returned to the fold after stints elsewhere, while Ray Lewington liked the Cottage so much he's returned twice since his initial spell – firstly as player-manager and currently as a member of the coaching staff.

Why do they, and we, love Fulham? Is it the picturesque Craven Cottage and its unique location – or something more? The word you may be looking for was coined by the club as its telegram address (and if you remember what a telegram is you're as old as I am!). Fulhamish has since entered the vernacular as a kind of all-encompassing adjective to cover the club's unorthodox and often frustrating progress. So it is with Fulhamish pleasure that we include Les Strong's account of the 1975 Cup Final as the Match of his Life, even though injury prevented him from playing in it!

Then we wanted Alan Mullery, the man whose name was indelibly painted on a Stevenage Road wall in most un-Fulhamish fashion, to tell us one of his stories, but, though willing, a forthcoming autobiography precluded his participation. Also, Rodney McAree, the Irishman who scored the goal that gave Fulham the first of their promotions at Carlisle in 1997 under Micky Adams, was impossible to get hold of until after the deadline had passed. Your editor is now well acquainted with the cleaner, barlady and caretaker at Dungannon Swifts, where Rod's playing and coaching career continues! Maybe next time…

The nature of players' memories tend to vary according to era and viewpoint. Many games chose themselves, either for a particular individual's performance or the fixture's relevance to Fulham history. While Gordon 'Ivor' Davies proudly chooses his first career hat-trick, the club was still relegated that season in Fulhamish fashion. But Steve Earle, whose account highlights the awe in which teenage players like himself viewed the Robsons and Haynes, overlooks his five goals against Halifax in favour of saving Fulham from top-flight disaster at Northampton in 1966 – ensuring George Cohen could look his World Cup team-mates in the eye a few months later!

Ray Lewington pinpoints a mid-1980s match which, though it will never loom large in the histories of either ourselves or Wolves, gave him the first inspiration to pursue a managerial career thanks to the tactical acumen of coach Ray Harford, while team-mate Roger Brown opts for the game that saw Fulham pack the Cottage with over 20,000 people to cheer them to promotion to the Second Division under Malcolm Macdonald in 1982. Roger's blood and guts performance that sank promotion rivals Lincoln led to a memorable dressing-room photo which says almost as much as the words…

The Cup Final campaign of 1975 provides not one but two interviews, and for that we make no apology. Fulham are probably the only club who would play a 20th anniversary game to celebrate a defeat, and until the recent rocket through the divisions fuelled by chairman Mohamed Al Fayed's munificence, the Wembley showpiece was still the abiding memory of most fans of middle age or above.

My elder son saw his first game against Barnet in 1995, age eight, but has since seen Rooney, Lampard, Henry and Owen regularly strutting their stuff at the Cottage – a stunning transformation in a decade. Playing in the Premiership against household names week in, week out, means a second volume of reminiscences shouldn't be too hard to compile if demand dictates. But past history, with all its trials and tribulations, has thrown up characters and stories the like of which we will never see again. Football has changed, and Fulham inevitably with it.

The interviews contained herein were the product of a team covering every era of Fulham support over the last half-century. Chris Mason first came to the Cottage in 1951 and was programme editor for a couple of seasons, while I (born 1955) was unfortunate enough to miss Johnny Haynes by a single match: I still get that sinking feeling when I recall the early-1970 line-up change, Barry Lloyd for Johnny Haynes. No offence, Barry…

Another Lloyd – David, the indefatigable editor of long-running fanzine *There's Only One F in Fulham* – has played a major role in getting this book off and running and is of similar vintage to myself, while the midfield quartet is completed by Patrick Mascall. Despite his relative youth, he clocked up eight years with the club, latterly as publications editor, before going freelance in the 2005 close season. His contacts naturally proved invaluable, and he was able to get players to talk with a frankness rarely granted to others.

If you need further evidence of Fulham's pull over its former players, consider the fact that when I encountered club record scorer Gordon Davies outside Villa Park in 2002 before the FA Cup semi-final between former clubs Fulham and Chelsea, his black and white tie made any question as to who he would be supporting superfluous. That game, for obvious reasons, doesn't make it into this book – we hope you enjoy the ones that have!

Michael Heatley
September 2005

Foreword

JOHNNY HAYNES Inside-forward 1952–1970

Goals, atmosphere, intensity, rivalry, giant-killings; just some of the ingredients of a truly great football match, and at Fulham there have been many. Naturally, it's thrilling to win by a big margin, but a flood of goals isn't a prerequisite for a classic encounter. For me, nothing beats a game hanging in the balance until the dying seconds, especially when it's a Cup tie or a promotion decider. The significance of a single strike can be enough to etch a game into history forever.

The Cup semi-finals of 1975, Lincoln in '82 – so much was at stake and yet these games could have gone either way. That's what had fans on the edge of their seats and forged such indelible memories in their hearts. When the whistle blows and you've won, there's nothing quite like it. When you're on the losing side, it's a bitter pill to swallow. Either way, being part of such classics – for player and fan alike – is a special and unique experience

But games can be classics for a variety of reasons. The prospect of relegation has the capacity to create drama to rival the glory of cups and promotion. Sometimes the most highly-billed games are nothing but an anti-climax, with each side so fearful of defeat. Conversely, a game with nothing more riding on it than three simple points can be unexpectedly propelled to the stuff of legend.

I was fortunate enough to have been involved in some incredible clashes during my time at Fulham. Newcastle in the Cup in 1956, the famous semi-finals against Manchester United in 1958, the great escape at Northampton in 1966 – they are just three included in this fantastic collection in which I'm proud to have played a part. The Newcastle game lurched from one extreme to the other as we turned a 3-0 deficit into a 4-3 lead before their two late goals knocked us out. Against Manchester United at Villa Park in '58 we were a goal down and had clawed our way back to 2-1 before Bobby Charlton equalised to force a replay. At Northampton in '66 we came back from behind twice to win 4-2 and stave off relegation. The vivid memory of those occasions will stay with me forever.

Match of My Life brings together accounts of twelve legendary Fulham games from the last six decades, as told by those individual players whose names have become synonymous with each occasion. From my old friends Tosh Chamberlain, George Cohen and Steve Earle, via the likes of Les Strong, Gordon Davies and Roger Brown, to the more recent generation of Lee Clark and Sean Davis, this collection of stories will provide readers with a unique players-eye view of events that have gone down in Fulham folklore.

I feel immensely proud of my twenty years at Fulham Football Club and I am delighted to introduce this book. There is no better way to document such significant episodes in the history of English football's most unique institution.

Johnny Haynes
September 2005

Dedication

The book is dedicated to Jim Sims – sadly no longer with us, but a man whose idiosyncratic interviews with former players made half-time entertainment superfluous in the 1980s when he wrote in the programme as Lilliewhite. He is a team member in spirit.

TOSH CHAMBERLAIN
LEFT-WING 1951–1965

BORN 11th July 1934, Camden Town
SIGNED July 1951 from ground staff
FULHAM CAREER 204 games, 64 goals
HONOURS Promotion to First Division 1958-59
LEFT Free transfer to Dover, May 1965

A pacy left-winger with a venomous shot, Trevor (Tosh to his friends) was a school chum of Johnny Haynes and was instrumental in Haynes signing for Fulham. The two linked well on the left side of Fulham's attack for over a decade. After scoring with his first kick in a Fulham shirt in November 1954, Tosh became a man of the people and was often to be found during a game cadging a cigarette from or chatting to spectators. Tosh is still very much part of the Cottage social scene, though now into his seventies.

Fulham 4 v Newcastle United 5

FA Cup Fourth Round
Saturday 28 January 1956

Craven Cottage
Attendance 39,200

"The best football match of all time." Tosh Chamberlain

Teams

Ian Black	1	Bobby Simpson
Tom Wilson	2	Arnold Woollard
Robin Lawler	3	Alf McMichael
Norman Smith	4	Bob Stokoe
Gordon Brice	5	Tommy Paterson
Eddie Lowe	6	Tom Casey
Jimmy Hill	7	Jackie Milburn
Bobby Robson	8	Reg Davies
Bedford Jezzard	9	Vic Keeble
Johnny Haynes	10	Bill Curry
Tosh Chamberlain	11	Bobby Mitchell

Chamberlain 39, 68, 70	**Scorers**	Milburn 16, Stokoe 20
Hill 73		Casey 25, Keeble 78, 82

Referee: J Mitchel

IT'S HARD TO credit that this game took place 50 years ago – where's all that time gone? I don't dwell on the game (there's much more to life than that!), but when you think back it's hard not to get taken in with all the excitement of the occasion. We'd beaten Notts County away 1-0 with a Johnny Haynes goal in the third round and then in the next round been drawn at home against the FA Cup holders. Newcastle were, without doubt, one of the top sides of the day. They'd won the Cup three times in five years. We were a decent Second Division outfit, but to draw them at home was a big thing for all of us, and the excitement, and nerves, increased as the day of the big match approached.

This was my first cup-tie. I'd played six League games for the club the previous season, but Charlie Mitten had worn the number 11 shirt for the most part. Having signed as a professional in July 1951 aged 17, I'd had to do my National Service, so I missed quite a few games because of that. My first Fulham game was against Lincoln in November 1954 and I scored with my very first kick in the opening minute. I couldn't believe my luck! Anyway, with Charlie a regular starter I didn't get a game for Fulham in 1955-56 until the end of November, and wished I hadn't bothered as we went down 7-0 at Anfield. But from then I was more or less a first choice on the left wing under Frank Osborne. Charlie was getting on by then and it was one of those natural progressions as a good old pro made way for fresh blood.

We'd been playing very well at home in the lead-up to the game – I recall we had two 4-1 home wins on the bounce against Swansea and Middlesbrough and then beat West Ham 3-1 the week before the tie. So it wasn't simply a case of us raising our game against the Cup-holders. In fact we had some decent names in our line-up, too. Our right-back Tom Wilson was a good player, then we had Robin Lawler at left-back, he was a terrific player as well. Big Gordon Brice played at centre-half and had a great game – you certainly couldn't blame him for the way we leaked five goals.

Newcastle, of course, were a top team and they'd won the Cup in 1951 and 1952 as well as 1955. Reg Simpson was a good keeper, Woollard was a decent full-back and Bob Stokoe was a top-class performer. But their attacking players were awesome. "Wor" Jackie Milburn was something else. Just recently we've seen something like 15,000 people turn up to see new-signing Michael Owen being paraded around St James's Park, but when poor Jackie died in 1988 all of Newcastle lined the city's streets to pay their respects! He was such a big man and a truly great player.

I was still something of a kid, remember. One of my faults was that I'd get carried away by who we were playing against. And if you were up against Mitchell or Milburn, or were all set to be on the same pitch as Tom Finney or Stanley Matthews, it was very difficult not to stand in awe of them. It was amazing to think that I was going to be out there with these footballing geniuses. Football was so very different then, of course. And it's not all changed for the better.

Anyway, here I was about to be on the same pitch as "Wor" Jackie Milburn and Bobby "Dazzler" Mitchell – to name but two of Newcastle's great side. I have to admit the tummy was rolling a bit, even more so when we went out into the din of the crowd. It was the biggest attendance I'd ever seen at the Cottage. And what a noise they made! In those days it was okay for the crowd to spill over onto the pitch surrounds. There were that many there – 39,200 was the listed figure – that not only were there people around the pitch, but many were locked out too. And here was I about to be a part of it all.

In fact, with so many sat on the touchline I was going to be fairly intimately involved with a lot of them! I always used to talk to the crowd anyway, perhaps not so much in my younger days, but on this occasion I almost had no choice. I always knew that it was the supporters who paid my wages so I felt it a duty to entertain them and make them feel involved. Which, of course, is a totally different concept to the way the game is played today.

Some people would suggest that I was too much of a wag over the years, but I'd always insist that, as it was the spectators who paid my wages, I had to do my bit for them. Obviously the bottom line was always doing my very best for Fulham Football Club and to help them win as many games as was possible, but I never lost sight of the fact that I was there to entertain the people and to give them some pleasure – whether that meant nipping over into the Enclosure to share a cigarette with a supporter or simply some running banter. Then again, it probably wasn't in my best interests to snap the corner flag in two when I mistimed a corner kick – the fans all laughed on that occasion, but it bleedin' well hurt!

We ran down onto the pitch for the start of the game and the crowd noise was astonishing – the roar was really deafening. I was hoping I could control my nerves. Once you're on the park and you've had a few kicks of the ball then all of that melts away into the background somehow. We knew we had to play to our strengths. In my case that meant using my speed and making the most of the fact that I could hit the ball hard. I had the bonus, of course, of having a wonderful inside-forward. If I made a run and got myself into various positions I could be sure that Johnny would find me.

Johnny Haynes was a world-class player. And he was a magnificent guy to have in your side. He could be overbearing at times, but only because of his supreme ability. Not that I stood any nonsense from John – we'd been mates since schooldays and our friendship blossomed because of his mother and father, who treated me like another son, so if he cussed at me I'd cuss back at him. Only more so. There was one occasion when we were having a swearing match on the pitch and the referee marched over all set to caution the pair of us. We simply said that we always talked to each other like that and he walked away laughing.

We weren't necessarily daunted by facing Newcastle. We were full of respect for their line-up, but were up for the clash. Trouble is, we suddenly found ourselves three goals behind. Jackie Milburn got the first after about 16 minutes. Four minutes after that Bob Stokoe saw his shot fly in off Tom Wilson, then Tom Casey slid through the mud to finish off a flowing Newcastle attack. It was tough on us as we'd opened quite brightly, but they demonstrated what a good side they were. Then I got a goal back with my trusty left peg about five minutes before half-time. I can't remember too much about it if I'm honest, except that I saw the two sticks, hit the ball and in it went. By the time we got into the dressing room at the break we'd built up a little more confidence. Enough for us to suggest that "if they can get three goals then so can we."

For my second after 68 minutes, Johnny hit a good ball through; I gave it a decent crack and the next thing it was in the net! Suddenly we were getting excited – and Jimmy Hill, cor blimey, was running all over the park, popping up left, right and centre. We were really in the game. In fact two minutes later I fired in our third and we were not only in the game, but now looking the likely winners. Three-apiece after being three down, and all three from my left foot – that's the stuff of dreams, isn't it?

One of the funniest parts of the Newcastle encounter involved the handicapped spectators who sat at the edge of the pitch in their wheelchairs. Every time we scored as I ran back to my position on the wing I was in real danger of getting hurt as I had to dodge a stack of crutches and walking sticks flying through the air in all directions! And if we had managed to win the game what a joy it would have been for those wonderful people – and all the other super Fulham supporters.

The game was a pulsating, almost claustrophobic affair, and there's no doubt that the crowd lifted us. The noise was incredible – so much so that it's hard to put it into words. It was the crowd as much as anyone on the park that lifted us once we'd gone three-down. There's no doubt the crowd can play a big part in a game. It's a two-way thing, I know, and they need to be lifted themselves at times, whether through an incident or knowing that their team is giving their all. A crowd needs to be entertained and to have leaders on the pitch. And that's as valid today as it was in my day.

It wasn't all going our way, though. I scored another; at least I thought I had – I beat the full-back before putting the ball in the net, but the linesman's given me offside. It was a ridiculous decision, and one that probably cost us dearly. But, do you know, I still see that linesman today – he went on to become one of this country's most respected referees and was in charge of the 1974 World Cup Final. A certain Jack Taylor, the Wolverhampton butcher. Every time I see him, I tell him "You definitely worked a flanker back in 1956!" The referee actually gave the goal, but scrubbed it after seeing Jack's flag. All I can say is that Taylor's eyesight certainly improved over the years!

Then we did score our fourth goal through Jimmy Hill. We were ahead with about 15 minutes left. I think it's fair to say he was a very happy man at that moment. If they'd have opened the gates as he went on his victory jink he'd have headed off to Putney and beyond – we couldn't hold him! It was amazing. Suddenly we were leading 4-3. How could that have happened? It was one hell of a cup-tie.

Frankie Penn, our trainer, bless his heart – great guy and terrific trainer – starts sticking his fingers up giving us signals. We're all thinking, "what the dickens is all that about?", but he was trying to tell us there were only a few minutes left to play. Remember the officials didn't add time on as they do today. Three or four minutes usually meant just that. We were pretty much in control with a little over 10 minutes on the clock. Even now it seems impossible that any side could score twice in those closing stages.

Play our cards right and we're home and dry. Defend properly and we're ruddy home and dry against the mighty Newcastle!

But it didn't work out like that. Their winger, Mitchell, picked two balls up out wide and put in a couple of crosses and Keeble forced them in. Our goalkeeper Ian Black...say no more! I still say Ian was airborne as he took one of those crosses and was barged into the net so, by rights, that goal should not have stood. In my days such barges were allowed (so very different to today's game), but only if the keeper had his feet on the deck.

Then again, it was so close to full-time, and all Ian had to do (and yes, I know it's all too easy to criticise someone for something that happened half a century ago) with one of those goals was to touch the ball over the crossbar. That in itself would have eaten up a minute or two as the corner-kick was taken. The game would have been over. With us going into those last few minutes, the very worst case scenario should have been a replay back at their place. And their gates were more than 60,000 so just imagine the gate money for Fulham if we'd played up there. But no, Ian tries to catch both crosses as they came down, Keeble hits him and ball into the net and we're out!

In fact when I saw the photo of that goal which features in this book, it really brought all those memories flooding back. There's Ian lying on his back, desperately trying to grab the ball, which has just bounced over the line. Gut-wrenching.

I saw Frank Osborne's face as we trooped off the pitch, and he wasn't best pleased. Being big-headed, I knew he wasn't going to have a go at me because I'd done my job; I'd stuck the ball into the Newcastle net three times. Well, four times actually. And I couldn't have done much more than that. Even if I'd had a bad game as a player, I'd done what you have to do as a forward and that's score a few goals. I knew that someone who'd been playing at the back was up for copping the flak.

It's gone down in Fulham's history as not only a truly great cup-tie, but probably the best game ever seen at Craven Cottage. I can tell you that immediately afterwards the only way to describe our feelings was "utter despondency". We'd "won" the game, only to throw it away. There's no other way to sum it up. I realised there'd be some arguing in the dressing room afterwards, with Ian bearing the brunt of the comments, so, being just a kid, I was in and out of the bath and off, quick as I could. There was very little time to think about my hat-trick or any of the positives such as our thrilling comeback; I just wanted to be out of it before the arguments set off.

A number of the guys were having a right go at Ian. In some ways you could understand it. Some people get carried away in the sense that they're so dedicated to what they're doing. And it's true that, had we taken such a decent scalp, then we'd have been in with a great chance of getting somewhere. In the end, exciting match or not, it was a terrible way to lose. And a lousy way to go out of the Cup.

Let's not forget that Ian Black was a Scottish international goalkeeper. My main thought about Ian is that he probably wasn't crazy enough to be a really top-class keeper. They say goalkeepers are crazy, but Ian was more of a gentleman. I still see Ian now – he only lives down the road from me – and he's still something of a quiet person. All the other keepers I knew, such as Hughie Kelly and Dougie Flack, were all a bit nutty, whereas Ian was much quieter and more reserved. Lovely fellow for all that.

Newcastle's Cup defence eventually ended with a 2-0 home defeat by Sunderland in the quarter-final. When I heard that result I couldn't help but think "That could have been us."

We're all so very different as individuals. But it was a marvellous time to play for Fulham and we had a great bunch of players, many of whom I'm still in touch with on a regular basis. Take Johnny. A lot of people would say, "Cor, didn't he used to ruck you?!" And he did. But it's only when he was on the park, and when he was totally wrapped up in the game and concentrating so very hard on matters going on all around him. People would ask: 'What's he like to play with?' Well, sometimes he was an absolute nightmare, because he was so engrossed and I'd often end up getting a rollicking for nothing.

But then, you see, you'd come in the dressing room and, all right, you might have a moan for five minutes or so. The trouble is, unfortunately, that whatever it was that you're having a moan about, you can't turn back the clock and put it right. All you can do is try to do the right thing next time you're on the park. You'd have a flashpoint, of course you would, when someone would say "Christ, why didn't you do this, that or the other?", but once you'd had your shower or your bath it was all over. And it was no different in most dressing rooms up and down the country.

As far as the Newcastle result was concerned it was a case of coming in for training on the Monday and just getting on with things. We were pretty flat in spirit for two or three days, though, and we didn't actually win another game for over a month after that. You'd be sitting in groups at times agreeing that we should have been in the fifth round. At worst we should have been training hard for a replay at Newcastle, but it didn't happen and we had to get on with it. It had been such a heady encounter, but we'd let it slip after making such a wonderful recovery.

We soon got to realise the magnitude of that particular cup-tie. Sure we were upset. And of course we gradually got over it. From my point of view, I've said earlier that I didn't really know for sure how I'd performed except that I'd got three goals to my name. But people were talking for weeks afterwards to me about this game. It was non-stop. It must have been wonderful for the spectators to watch with so many thrills and spills. And, of course, 50 years later people are still talking about it.

As and when I go to Fulham today, I get so many people (the older ones, naturally!) come up to me and ask "Do you remember the Newcastle game?" It's lovely, it really is. It's always Newcastle, too, even though there were plenty of other decent matches in my long time at the club. So, obviously, it was an exciting game and it's great to talk to supporters about it, and anything else for that matter. The game was a special one for me and all of the players that day. It wasn't just a case of me getting a hat-trick, they all played brilliantly. To come back so well against a team that seemed to have all the answers was a terrific effort. We frightened the life out of Newcastle, that's for sure.

One of our guys had been pretty desperate to play. Bobby Robson had been out with an injury picked up a couple of weeks before, but he got his chance when Arthur Stevens was injured; they pushed Jimmy Hill to outside-right and brought in Bobby at inside-forward. He was dying to play against the Geordies, being one himself. Bobby was a good player at Fulham, but in my opinion he became a better one after he moved to West Brom and switched from inside-forward to wing-half. In fact, that's when he won his England caps.

Then there was Jimmy. One thing you could bank on with Jimmy Hill was when the whistle blew, whether for the start of a game or simply for training, he'd run and run and never stop until the very end. He had incredible stamina. He must have had unbelievable lungs. It makes me tired just thinking about him flying all over the place!

Up front we had Beddy Jezzard leading the attack; a great player to have there from a winger's point of view. You could whip in a cross and Beddy would go in for the ball with a wholehearted challenge. He was fast and didn't mind taking a bit of punishment.

Then at the heart of our team was Johnny. I suppose had I been any other young kid in the Fulham ranks I'd have found him a daunting character. But we'd built up this relationship from our schooldays. In our younger days I was bigger than him so I guess that why I found it so easy to stand up to him. We had a great friendship and it was through this that John came to Fulham. He could have gone to Arsenal or to Tottenham, but he chose Fulham as I was there.

For all of his ways, Johnny was an absolute dream to play with. What a talent! We were having a technical talk at the club one day and one young player asked Ron Greenwood about John's qualities. Ron said that John was lucky to be blessed with "peripheral vision". The youngster asked: "What's peripheral vision?" And Georgie Cohen butted in and said: "It means he's got eyes up his arse"! But that was Johnny. He could pass and size up situations like no-one else.

There were one or two things that annoyed me about John, given all his talent. One was that he didn't shoot enough. In my opinion he should have scored more goals. I know he scored plenty for the club over the years, but he had such a fantastic technique and such mastery of the football that I feel he should have gone for goal a bit more often. He had a hell of a drive on him and a magical half-volley.

As for his range of passing, well that was something else. They say Beckham can pass the ball around the park, but John was a far superior player with a far superior range of passing. He did it with the old leather footballs, don't forget, not these plastic balloons of today. John's vision and awareness was second to none. He could hit a wonderfully weighted pass and could see, or sense, the moves as they developed. I used to drive him mad at times. Sometimes I'd sit on the touchline and talk to the spectators. I'd probably get the sack for doing that today, but, like I said, I loved to involve the Fulham people. Meantime John would be doing his conkers of course. Especially if a pass intended for me had gone into touch because I'd gone "missing".

Looking back we had a side that really ought to have got out of that Second Division much sooner than we did. As the team evolved, on paper we had a team that was as good as any side in the League. What about this as a line-up: Macedo, Cohen, Langley, Mullery, Bentley, Lowe, Stevens, Robson, Jezzard, Haynes and yours truly as number 11? And yet we never really reached the heights that we should have done. There was one year that we went ten or twelve games without losing at the start of the season and we still didn't finish in the top places.

But it's a funny game, football. Everyone raves about the Newcastle game and yet just the week before that match I put in a performance that, for me, was much better in football terms. Against West Ham I was in really top form. I was up against full-back John Bond; you may remember him as the bejewelled manager of Norwich and Manchester City in the 1970s and 80s. He'd soon had enough and switched flanks! I was on the scoresheet along with Beddy Jezzard and Jimmy Hill. It was a lot less frantic that day and I had a lot more time to think about things, and I managed to take the right options more often than not. Towards the end of the season I grabbed another hat-trick in a 4-0 win over Doncaster. But, for all that, we eventually finished ninth.

In all my years at Fulham we had a terrific comradeship. It really was a friendly club, make no mistake about that. Some might say that we were too bloody friendly, seeing as we muddled about in the middle of the Second Division for so long. But who's to know? And the relationship with the Fulham supporters of the time remains fresh today, which makes all that larking about so very worthwhile. It's heart-warming to be remembered after all those years.

I still see a lot of the players from those days. We tend not to talk about the Newcastle game amongst ourselves, great though it was – but it's all too easy to compare the way the game's played today, what with their lush, bowling-green pitches as opposed to, more often than not, the mud-heaps we had to play on. Ken Jones, the veteran reporter, was saying not too long ago that the strong, lasting comradeship we had – and still have – isn't there today. If that's the case, more fool them.

The funny thing about that cup-tie was that, the following week, there was a bloody great picture of me taking up the whole of the back page of the Arsenal programme. We weren't playing them, either! It was captioned something like: "Trevor Chamberlain, the unluckiest player in football – a hat-trick against the FA Cup holders, yet he still finished on the losing side." Unlucky? Maybe so. But I've been very lucky in so many other ways.

GEORGE COHEN MBE
RIGHT-BACK 1955–1969

BORN   23rd October 1937, Kensington, London
SIGNED   1955 as schoolboy
FULHAM CAREER   459 games, 60 goals
HONOURS   Promotion to First Division 1958-59
LEFT   Retired through injury, April 1969

George may be most famous for his exploits as a World Cup winning England player, but as a one-club man in the domestic game, he appeared in more matches for Fulham than all but four other men. Almost ever present from 1958 to 1967, George's great ability to recover quickly against speedy wingers prevented many goals, and he is still remembered as one of the club's best ever defenders. Manchester United's legendary winger George Best described him as "the best full-back I ever played against".

Fulham 2 v Manchester United 2

FA Cup Semi-final
Saturday 22 March 1958

Villa Park
Attendance 69,745

Fulham just fail to clinch their first ever place in a Wembley final after taking on the Busby Babes in a post-Munich surge of emotion

Teams

Tony Macedo	1	Harry Gregg
George Cohen	2	Bill Foulkes
Jim Langley	3	Ian Greaves
Roy Bentley	4	Freddie Goodwin
Joe Stapleton	5	Ronnie Cope
Robin Lawler	6	Stan Crowther
Roy Dwight	7	Colin Webster
Jimmy Hill	8	Ernie Taylor
Arthur Stevens	9	Alex Dawson
Johnny Haynes	10	Bobby Charlton
Tosh Chamberlain	11	Mark Pearson

Stevens 13, Hill 39	**Scorers**	Charlton 12, 45

Referee: C Kingston

Fulham 3 v Manchester United 5

FA Cup Semi-final replay
Wednesday 26 March 1958

Highbury
Attendance 38,258

Teams

Tony Macedo	1	Harry Gregg
George Cohen	2	Bill Foulkes
Jim Langley	3	Ian Greaves
Roy Bentley	4	Freddie Goodwin
Joe Stapleton	5	Ronnie Cope
Robin Lawler	6	Stan Crowther
Roy Dwight	7	Colin Webster
Jimmy Hill	8	Ernie Taylor
Arthur Stevens	9	Alex Dawson
Johnny Haynes	10	Bobby Charlton
Tosh Chamberlain	11	Shay Brennan

Stevens 27, Chamberlain 38	**Scorers**	Dawson 14, 34, 65
Dwight 73		Brennan 44, Charlton 90

Referee: C Kingston

"HAVE YOU EVER thought of being a full-back, sonny?" came the question in a thick Scottish brogue. "No…" I said. "Well you have now." In that moment, Fulham's Manager Dugald Livingstone changed my life for ever. I was 16 years old. Two years later I would be playing in an FA Cup semi-final against the mighty Manchester United in front of nearly 70,000 people and within a decade I would have won the World Cup as England's right-back.

I was born in Fulham, about a mile away from the ground in what was then known as Walham Green, now Fulham Broadway. My family were a mixture of Fulham and Chelsea supporters. I went to a school called Fulham Central, which is now called Henry Compton. It was a terrific school for sports back then. Their philosophy was to get youngsters interested in sport to help develop a sense of discipline which would then carry over to academic work. One of our coaches was a man by the name of Ernest Shepherd who had close ties with Fulham Football Club. He'd been a player himself and had played for Fulham between 1946 and 1948. I made a real impression on Ernest, although I think that was more because I could out-run him than anything else.

I was about 15 at the time, but it wasn't my burning ambition to be a footballer. I mean, I loved the game, but it wasn't until Ernie came along that I realised I had a chance to make the grade. Ernie insisted that I'd be better off at a club like Fulham because he knew they'd take more interest in younger players like me than say, Chelsea. And he was right. Chelsea had been known for years as a club that had tried to buy success, something which isn't just true of today, so it made a lot more sense to join the Cottagers.

So I gave it a try, and after my O-levels I left school and joined Fulham as an amateur, playing for the reserves in the South East Counties League. I started as a winger. It was only by accident that I ended up a defender. I was playing in a game and our left-back got injured. So the manager, Dug Livingstone, put me there as cover. I was marking an England amateur international by the name of Pat Neil, who was a bit of a flier. But I took care of him and that obviously impressed Livingstone.

From that moment on, he had me in every afternoon schooling me in the art of defending. Football is a game of movement, it's about width and depth and it was with Dugald that I learnt about positional play as a defender. He drilled into me that, as a full back, I was primarily a defender. His instruction was always, "learn how to defend first, and let the attacking side follow." But he also taught me about things like overlaps and how to run on to balls, thereby keeping the game fluid, rather than waiting to receive the ball. From Dugald I learnt that overlaps were actually very easy but very effective moves to make, but that you just had to bide your time for the right opportunity. If you did, you'd find yourself making just two or three overlaps a game, but to devastating effect. They were lessons that stayed with me for the rest of my career.

Fulham was a wonderful place for a youngster like me. The senior players and coaches were devoted to helping us develop, as players and as people. Livingstone had been a full-back himself playing for Celtic, Everton and Tranmere and, along with the help of former Fulham and England player Joe Bacuzzi, who was Reserve Team Coach, and senior players like full-back Tom Wilson and half-back Roy Bentley, moulded me into the player I became. It couldn't have been a more perfect grounding.

My ascent was rapid. I signed professional at 17 and made my debut at home to Liverpool in March 1957, but that was the only game I was to play that season. It was the following campaign, 1957-58, when my career really began to take off. Not from the start of the season, I hasten to add. I was pulled into the side for a home match against Huddersfield in the November following some injuries in the camp. We were an ageing side at the time and I think that Livingstone had been keen to inject some youthful energy into proceedings; this gave him the perfect opportunity to do just that. But I must have impressed. From that moment on, I kept my place and didn't miss a game in a season which took us all the way to those legendary FA Cup semi-final appearances against Manchester United.

My introduction to the side was one of three main changes implemented by Livingstone in '57/58. Also given his first-team baptism was a young goalkeeper who would go on to be a regular for many years, Elio, better known as Tony, Macedo. But Livingstone also made a shrewd tactical move, switching the legendary Roy Bentley, recently arrived from Chelsea where he had been the skipper of their 1955 title winning side, from striker to wing-half so we could benefit from his know-how, craft and vision rather than his fading pace.

The three changes certainly had an impact – at least I like to think they did. By the December we'd had a great run of form, and a draw and six wins had even sent us top of the Second Division for a while. As always, the New Year kicked off with the FA Cup third round. But, based on the experience of the previous few seasons, nobody could have even imagined the thrilling climax that would emerge. The 1950s hadn't been a great Cup decade for Fulham. We reached the last eight in 1951, but, other than exiting to holders Newcastle in round four in 1956 as Tosh has already mentioned, the club had otherwise always gone out at the first time of asking.

The campaign started with an insalubrious home tie against non-League Yeovil. Non-league they may have been, but Yeovil had become renowned for being cup fighters and their reputation as giantkillers surpassed all others after knocking out First Division Sunderland back in 1949. Of course, Alec Stock, who would later manage Fulham to Wembley, was Yeovil's player-manager for that game. So with a pedigree like that we would have to be careful. Despite the gulf in status, it was still goalless at half-time. With all due respect to Yeovil, though, it really should have been a convincing victory and, by the time the final whistle sounded, we'd put four past them and were in the hat for the next round. We had a great deal of experience in the side that season which was clearly paying dividends and the introduction of young Tony Macedo in goal gave us something different too. He was very agile, quick around the box, was brimming with confidence and added a new dimension to the side.

In the next two rounds we faced Charlton and West Ham. Like us, both were London clubs and both were Division Two promotion challengers, so rivalry was rife. It took us two attempts to beat Charlton, but we managed to turn over the Hammers at Upton Park in one go. It was that man Macedo who was the difference. He must have pulled out over twenty world-class saves in those ties. There was one in particular where he seemed to dive so high, it looked as if he was literally just below the cross-bar, totally horizontal to it. Tony's reactions were second to none when he was on form.

Some of us were lucky to have even made it to Upton Park, having escaped injury in a car accident a few days before. In those days we used to go on these wonderful week-long training camps down in Worthing. Dugald would say to us, "Sunday and Monday are for you. The rest of the week is for the club." So we used to go and play a day or two's golf before knuckling down to some hard work. I'll never forget Worthing's golf course – it was so hilly! But for some reason or other, every time we came back from one of these camps we did really well. So they kept sending us on them.

It was a few days before the fifth round tie against West Ham. We were travelling back to London from Worthing in a Humber Pullman, a huge old tank of a car, driven by the owner of our hotel. The boot was stacked with kit, of course, and being the middle of winter the weather was awful. Somehow the driver lost control in the icy fog and we ended up skidding into a ditch by the side of the road. Bruised and shaken, and still sheltering from the elements in the car, we managed to get out of the ditch with the help of a breakdown truck. But in the process we ended up careering into the ditch on the other side of the road! It was a particularly nasty experience and we were lucky to get out unscathed. But we lived to tell the tale and the Worthing trip weaved its magic once more.

Having disposed of our two London rivals we got a kind home draw to Bristol Rovers in the quarter-final, whom we disposed of 3-1. By then we'd really established some rhythm and were playing well. In this same run of form we beat Grimsby in the League 6-0 and Doncaster 6-1 away from home. Winning is definitely a habit, and we were certainly getting used to it.

But although confidence was very high, none of us were getting ideas beyond our station, especially when the mighty Manchester United came out of the hat for the semi-final. They were a different kettle of fish to anything we had faced along the way and, although we were confident in our own abilities, the draw certainly put paid to any notions of taking a Wembley appearance for granted.

However there was another, more sinister dimension to this particular semi-final. Sir Matt Busby's legendary Busby Babes had been decimated by the Munich air crash only a matter of seven weeks before. I'll never forget hearing the news of the disaster. It was after training one day. I was playing snooker with Frank Osborne who was by then Fulham's General Manager. The phone rang and he picked it up. I don't know who it was, but as they spoke Frank's eyes filled with tears as he was told of the deaths of numerous United players. Being a teenager still, I certainly wasn't as emotional as Frank. But I was still aware of the magnitude of what had happened. How could I not have been? Some of the country's most talented players had died on that infamous night.

The subsequent resurrection of the Busby Babes has become part of football folklore. But when you look back now, that FA Cup semi-final against Fulham was really an integral stage of the beginning of that process. Because Manchester United had lost so many players to the tragedy in Munich, the Football Association granted them special dispensation to sign more than half a team's worth of players who were already cup-tied so they could rebuild their squad. They'd defeated Sheffield Wednesday 3-0 in the fifth round in the first game after the crash. Famously the programme for that game showed an empty United team line-up as no-one had much of an idea who would be playing. United pulled through with their rag-tag and bobtail side of hastily-signed pros and a glimpse at the strength of feeling which surrounded United at this time can be seen when in the quarter-final they defeated West Brom after replay, but then lost the rearranged league game against the same opponents three days later 4-0 at home. United were seriously up for the Cup this year, determined to win it for their dead team-mates.

In a peculiar way, the plane crash was the coming of age of Bobby Charlton. While he was always part of the orchestra, so to speak, he was still a youngster. But out of the ashes of Munich, this young man stepped up and came to the fore. It was one of those strange twists of fate that unexpectedly and, possibly prematurely, put this huge responsibility on a young fellow who was only two years older than me. He was already an up-and-coming star, no question. But there is no doubt that Munich projected him a few steps further along the road than he would have been at that time.

In the build-up to the semi-final at Villa Park, Bobby was a major talking point in the Fulham camp. We knew we would have to find a way to contain him and that it would be very dangerous to allow him a free shot on goal. But we had a lot of confidence in each other. Our spirit was tremendous, we all got along royally and we were by no means daunted at the prospect of facing Manchester United.

The team that started the semi-final was the same XI that had played in every round along the way. This was the days before substitutes were allowed, so the strongest eleven played every game provided they were fit. As mentioned, in goal was the irrepressible Tony Macedo. Tony and I were the babes of side, both having risen to prominence that season. In fact he got in the side slightly after me, but that was only because his early times at Fulham were hampered by National Service with the RAF. He was only a month older than I was, but that month was the cut-off point for a compulsory stint with the Forces and as a result, I'd missed it by the skin of my teeth! Of everyone in the team, Tony was the individual most responsible for us getting to the semi-final. He had been outstanding all the way, and it was most ironic that a rare bad performance in the replay would be our ultimate undoing.

My fellow full-back was Jimmy Langley. He came to us via Brighton and Leeds and was one of the great six-yard area defenders. At times his positional play left much to be desired – in fact he got away with murder! But around the area he was one of the best I've seen. He had almost elastic legs and was so quick into the tackle. Good in the air, an outstanding penalty-taker and the owner of one of the longest throws I've ever seen!

Roy Bentley had come to us from Chelsea. In my opinion he was jettisoned by Ted Drake far too early. The experience they lost when they let Roy go was irreplaceable as far as Chelsea were concerned. He had the most wonderful positional sense which Dug Livingstone utilised to full effect when he switched Roy's position. Because he was my own hero, there wasn't much I wouldn't do for Roy. He had a tremendous unselfishness about him and was always there for advice – invaluable to a youngster in my position.

The other two half-backs were Joe Stapleton and Robin Lawler. Joe was a no-nonsense player. Hard, not overly fast, but with a great presence in the air. Solid, stoic, reliable, that was Joe. Robin was one of nature's true gentlemen and was a very calming player to have in the side. He didn't have a great deal of pace, unfortunately, but he was skilful. He was a very stable kind of character and rarely put a foot wrong.

On the right wing was Elton John's uncle, Roy Dwight. Not unlike Elton himself, Roy always looked a bit tubby, but he couldn't half hit a volley. Where most other players would bring down a ball, Roy would volley it! At inside-right was "the Rabbi", Jimmy Hill, who scored in every round en route to the semis that season. Jim was a hell of a worker and another who was always willing to share his knowledge with us youngsters. The one thing about Jimmy was that you couldn't miss him, and more to the point, he wouldn't allow himself to be missed! He was a great personality to have around the place and still is. He had this great enthusiasm and was in a rich vein of form during that Cup run.

Arthur Stevens was at centre-forward. We called him "Pablo", although I haven't the faintest idea why! He was one of the most skilful players I have ever come across. For a small man he was tremendous in the air and had two very good feet. He was lightning quick over 15 yards which gave us that vital injection of pace in the last third of the pitch. By this time he was coming towards the end of his career, but he was still an outstanding player – at times, even on a par with the great Stanley Matthews. That's how good I thought he was.

At inside-left was the Maestro himself, our captain, Johnny Haynes. Johnny was in his early twenties in March 1958, but was already a world class player even though he still hadn't even reached his peak. I make no secret of my admiration for Johnny. He was outstanding, simple as that. He was the greatest foot-to-ball footballer I've ever seen and his ability to read the game was second to none. To be honest, there wasn't much Johnny Haynes wasn't good at. As far as I am concerned he is up there with Pele and Beckenbauer as one of the all-time truly world class players.

On John's left was good old Tosh Chamberlain. You never really knew what was going to happen with Tosh. He'd hit a shot from 50 yards and it might well end up in the back of the net or the back of the stand – it was an each-way bet! He had the hardest shot I've ever seen, and if he hit one properly and on target the keeper had no chance. I remember playing Inter Milan in a friendly at the San Siro. Tosh took a free-kick from 35 yards and it literally screeched into the back of the net. The keeper just stood completely still. I don't think he even saw it. And there was this murmur around the ground as the ball hit the back of the net – not a roar, but a murmur of almost total surprise.

I couldn't imagine my time at Fulham without Tosh. He was one of the great entertainers who helped forge the famous character of the club. He was as forth-right as he was funny and he'd cripple you at times with his antics. I won't go into what they were – you couldn't really describe them, and you definitely couldn't print them!

The team was led by our manager, Dugald Livingstone, a man for which we all had the utmost respect. He was a very philosophical character, with a dry wit and a great knowledge of the game, and was always beautifully turned out. We had a lot of faith in him too. After all, he'd steered Newcastle to FA Cup glory only a couple of seasons before when they had defeated Manchester City 3-1. He'd also had the guts to leave the club when Newcastle's board had tried to interfere with his team selection. Dugald was a quiet disciplinarian. But people were different in those days. He didn't need to shout and holler at us back then because a level of respect existed that is perhaps absent now. We were all earning more money than if we'd have been working in other walks of life, even though it was poor pay by today's standards.

But there was a genuine appreciation of our position. The way I used to put it was that we ate better. It was the perfect metaphor. I loved ending up at places like the Midland Hotel in Manchester – the hors d'oeuvres was bigger than any main course you'd get at home! But we were aware of our good fortune and, perhaps most importantly, were incredibly grateful for it. But remember that many of these characters around the club in those days had been on active service in the Forces at some time or another. Joe Bacuzzi had been in North Africa. Roy Bentley had served on Russian convoys. It had a profound influence on people's values. There was a sense of respect and discipline among these fellows that filtered through the entire club.

Naturally there was a huge outpouring of public sympathy for Manchester United given the terrible events that had beset them. But when it came to the semi-final itself, the disaster had certainly not dampened support for Fulham from the general public, contrary to popular belief. We were still the Second Division minnows playing against the mighty First Division sharks. Of course the entire nation had been stunned by Munich. But in spite of that, we still had the public backing as the underdogs, and the support we received was absolutely tremendous. A staggering 69,700 people attended the match at Villa Park and I still maintain we had the majority of support. The place appeared to be draped almost exclusively in black and white and without question the vocal battle was won by the Fulham fans. Even my father, a Chelsea man at heart, broke ranks for the occasion. A few days before the game he had gone to a fancy dress shop in Hammersmith and bought a top hat which he took home and painted black and white!

Perhaps because I was still a teenager, much of the pre-game emotion passed me by. Considering I was about to step out in front of almost 70,000 people, I was even calm in the minutes immediately beforehand. But once I set foot on to the heavy mid-winter pitch it was impossible not to be affected by the intensity and scale of the occasion.

We didn't get off to the best of starts and, despite our discussions about the dangers of Bobby Charlton, he put United a goal up after 12 minutes. I was marking Colin Webster, one of the post-Munich draft. He wasn't giving me any problems, but at the same time I had to give him respect. Even if he had been brought in under unusual circumstances, he was still a Manchester United player all the same.

Although a goal down, we were playing well. With players like Johnny Haynes in the side, there was no way we were going to roll over at that early stage. It was centre-forward Arthur Stevens who got the equaliser, side-footing Jimmy Langley's cross into the net. Johnny Haynes was stupendous that day, both as a player and a leader. Late in the first half, turning defence into attack on the edge of our box, he found Dwight on the right. Roy's cross fell to Jimmy Hill who rode out a couple of fierce tackles before sliding the ball past Harry Gregg in the United goal. Suddenly we were 2-1 up against the mighty Manchester United.

Then disaster struck. Following a clash with United's giant teenage striker, Alex Dawson [who one scribe dubbed "the Red Devils' bull-necked battering ram"], Jimmy Langley was injured and carried off. These were the days before substitutes so the only solution was a reshuffle. With Jimmy still receiving treatment, Robin Lawler dropped to left-back. But United continued to turn the screw and perhaps inevitably, Bobby Charlton brought them level before Langley had re-entered the game. There were no goals in the second half. Johnny Haynes did find the net, but it was disallowed as a handball, not that I saw his hand anywhere near it. United put us under intense pressure in the closing stages, with Charlton and Dawson both going close and it was only the work of Tony Macedo, pulling off save after brilliant save, who earned us a second chance in the replay.

There was certainly no sense that we'd missed our big chance after the events at Villa Park. If anything we felt we understood Manchester United a little better. After all, they were something of an unknown quantity because they had so many new players in the team. We, on the other hand, were very much a unit who had played together for a long time and confidence was still high. The replay was held at Highbury four days later. It was the first time United had been back to the ground where just seven weeks earlier the Busby Babes had beaten Arsenal in a classic league game 5-4, the last match they had played in this country before Munich.

The replay was the first Fulham game to ever be televised, partly because it was held on a Wednesday afternoon and it did mean that many fans watched at home. Despite that there were queues all around Highbury as we arrived at the ground. There was a real sense that we could upset United and I think the crowd knew it too. This was now our city and we really fancied our chances. There was an expectant atmosphere and the gloomy fog which enveloped the ground as we took to the field added to the occasion too.

We weren't doing too badly to begin with, but, despite goals from Arthur Stevens and Tosh Chamberlain, we were still 3-2 down by half-time. Once again I was marking Colin Webster and he wasn't giving me too many problems, but we could all see that Tony Macedo was having a torrid time in goal.

One problem was that the giant teenage goal sensation, Alex Dawson, was having the game of his life. He bagged a hat-trick, in the process becoming the youngest hat-trick scorer [18 years and 33 days] at that stage of the competition. Not only that, but no-one has scored a treble in an FA Cup semi-final since.

He was helped, though, by Tony's goalkeeping. Tony was responsible for at least three of United's goals that afternoon in North London. Indeed one journalist described Tony's performance by claiming "he flapped and fumbled like a schoolgirl". I'm not sure he was quite that effeminate, but Tony was very much a confidence player – if he made that first catch you knew he'd be all right. If he didn't you knew he'd struggle, and he struggled that afternoon all right.

At 4-3 in the second half – Roy Dwight got our third – we were still in the game, and when Roy scored what looked like a perfectly good equaliser we thought the pendulum had swung our way, but the referee disallowed it. From there, United broke and Charlton scored their fifth with a cross-shot which completely wrong-footed Tony in our goal and really set the seal on a sorry day for him. That put the game out of reach for us and shattered any dreams of Fulham in a Wembley Final. It's funny, I don't remember a great deal about the replay and yet I remember so much about the first semi-final. But I think there's a simple explanation for that. The replay was such a disappointment that we all tried to put it out of our minds straight away. But the one aspect that none of us will forget were the mistakes that led to the goals.

It was ironic that Tony effectively cost us the game. Looking back, he deserves the bulk of the credit for taking us that far. Without Tony Macedo we wouldn't have made the semis. But because of Tony Macedo, we didn't make Wembley.

United went on to lose the Final to Bolton amidst a huge clamour about Nat Lofthouse shoulder-charging United's keeper Ray Wood into the net for United's second and clinching goal. That challenge effectively signalled the end of forwards being allowed to have contact with opposing goalkeepers and I think the sympathy surrounding United and their plight – and let's face it everyone in the country except Bolton fans wanted them to win the Cup final that year – played a huge part in that decision.

Meanwhile we turned our attention back to promotion from the Second Division. Like I said, winning is a habit and our League form had gone hand-in-hand with the Cup run. By the time the semi-final replay was over we were still sitting in fourth place with numerous games in hand over our rival promotion-chasers. It was a constant cycle of matches, but it was either that or training! From my point of view, I was so fanatical about football that it was just a pleasure to be playing so often. But ten fixtures in little over a month, including five in nine days, of which none were won, was just too much for us. The squad just didn't have the depth to cope with such a schedule.

In terms of numbers alone perhaps we had enough, but a lot of our players were either too young or too old. We weren't the kind of club who could afford to buy top-class players. We had to grow our own and relied on what our youth team could provide. In terms of players who could actually come in and do the business, we were too limited and we paid the price. In the end we only managed 11 points from 20, slipped to fifth and finished four points short of a promotion place. Progress in the Cup had come at the expense of going up.

Fulham had their best season in 25 years in 1957-58, both in the League and the Cup. But we still ended up empty-handed. In hindsight, perhaps that was representative of Fulham as a whole back then. I never actually won anything in my time at the Cottage, even though we went up to the First Division the following season and got to the FA Cup semi-finals again four years later, where we lost to Burnley after a replay. From 1957-58 I made over 450 appearances for Fulham in a one-club career. And, of course, playing for the Whites provided the platform for my England call-ups, which culminated in World Cup victory in 1966. To this day England haven't won a World Cup without the help of a Fulham player!

But when I cast my mind back over those days at Fulham, it's that 1958 FA Cup semi-final at Villa Park that really stands out for me. It epitomised such a wonderful era at the club. I was an 18-year-old local lad, playing the game I loved alongside some of my heroes – characters the likes of which will never be seen again. And, what's more, I didn't have to pay for my toffee apples down the North End Road!

STEVE EARLE
STRIKER 1961–1973

BORN   1st November 1945, Feltham, Middlesex
SIGNED   November 1961 as apprentice
FULHAM CAREER   327 games, 108 goals
HONOURS   Promotion to Second Division 1970-71
LEFT   Transferred to Leicester, November 1973; £70,000

A predatory striker with an eye for goal who could also play on the wing, Steve was under-rated by successive Fulham managers, but outlasted all his replacements until leaving for Leicester in late 1973 when financial demands forced his sale. Would probably have been close to international honours with a better team, but one goal in every three games over his Fulham career is no bad record.

Northampton Town 2 v Fulham 4

Division One
Saturday 23 April 1966

The County Ground
Attendance 24,523

*Earle's late treble wins Fulham this relegation six-pointer as the
Cottagers escape the top-flight trapdoor*

Teams

Norman Coe	1	Jack McLelland
John Mackin	2	George Cohen
Mike Everett	3	Brian Nichols
John Kurila	4	Bobby Robson
Terry Branston	5	John Dempsey
Joe Kiernan	6	Stan Brown
Harry Walden	7	Steve Earle
Graham Moore	8	Allan Clarke
George Hudson	9	Graham Leggat
Don Martin	10	Johnny Haynes
Barry Lines	11	Mark Pearson

Hudson 13, Kiernan 31   **Scorers**   Robson 19, Earle 65, 88, 90

Referee: J Taylor

I HAD A BIT of a love-hate relationship with the fans. I think most strikers do. My get-out was when I score I'm all right because you can go from the doghouse to the penthouse by scoring a goal. Fans really don't know how they affect players, how they can destroy them. I've played with some good youngsters who were absolutely destroyed by fans. If only they realised what they were doing...

One match, I forget who we were playing, I was having a nightmare and the crowd were giving me all sorts. There were only a few minutes left and I couldn't wait for the game to end. Lloydy [Barry Lloyd] was taking a corner down by the Hammersmith End and I was on the edge of the box. The ball came out to me; I just swung my left leg at it and absolutely roofed it. Bang – back of the net. Goal! I went from the doghouse to the penthouse in one kick. Play crap for 85 minutes, score a goal and all of a sudden you're a hero. It never ceases to amaze me!

But my career as a player is a different lifetime really. On leaving Fulham, I had four years with Leicester, after which I came over here to the States, where I've lived ever since. I never think about my playing days unless someone from England calls me. No-one in the States knows anything about Fulham: I don't speak about it, really. Obviously I can remember things, and when I read the Fulham books people send me I remember more, but there's a lot of goals I can't remember scoring!

I was born in Feltham and brought up in Whitton. Bedford Jezzard was the manager when I joined Fulham as an apprentice in 1961, signing pro in '63. I spent a couple of years in the reserves before making the breakthrough into the first team. I suppose it was to learn my trade as a forward.

I went through about six or seven managers. I never had anything in common with any of the older players. There was me, Freddie Callaghan and Rodney Marsh and we were teenagers, so young by comparison. All the others on the team, like Bobby Robson, were in their late twenties/early thirties, so we didn't do anything socially with them. All my friends were people I went to school with.

Training in those days wasn't like it is now – you'd probably have a practice match against the first team once a week. Nine times out of ten the reserves would do well, desperate to show they should be allowed to move up. But if you were in the first team, you hated those games. They didn't try 100 per cent in case you got injured. But us reserves were always eager to play. Johnny Key was in my position in the first team; I don't know if he got hurt or something, but Beddy called me in to make my full debut against Nottingham Forest. I did all right, could have scored a couple of times, and the next week I played against Blackpool and did score. Cut inside, shut my eyes, hit it and it went into the corner.

The following week I was due to be playing in the youth team at Hendon against Chelsea juniors. They pulled me off the field just before the morning kick-off and told me I was going to be playing against the Chelsea first team at Stamford Bridge that afternoon. I scored the winner that day, and that was the start of it all.

Funnily enough, my dad had taken me to watch Chelsea when was about 12, and I didn't like it, I came home. I didn't support anybody as a kid, I was always playing. I was taken on as a schoolboy at Brentford, when I was about 14. I used to train with them Tuesdays and Thursdays. I was playing for four teams every weekend: schoolboy, youth club and two men's teams in Hounslow on Saturday and Sunday. We didn't have the money to pay for me to watch games either, which was another reason, even in those days when football was much cheaper.

The season after my breakthrough came bad news – Vic Buckingham, who took over as manager. You could say that I didn't get on with him. He came in with all these different ideas and really didn't inspire me with any confidence. He never did anything creative on the training field, he left that to his assistant Ronnie Burgess, who he'd played with at Spurs.

I fell out with him when we were training and he didn't pick me for a year! We were playing a practice match against the reserves at Roehampton and I'll always remember what happened. The pitches there were all built up; they dipped down to another field at a lower level behind the goals. So if you hit the ball too hard it would go for miles. Marshy [Rodney Marsh] used to upset him by whacking it down there every day; training would stop till the ball was retrieved.

I remember Johnny Haynes put me through this one morning and I ran clean through the middle. Jack McLelland came sliding out of goal, but I took it round him, and I didn't want to hit it too hard because there were no nets up. I just flicked it, it hit the ruts on this frozen, hard field – we shouldn't even have been playing – and it hit the outside of the post and went down. I sort of sniggered and Vic went absolutely ballistic. I just told him to "Sod off" and I never spoke to him for a year, I didn't play, he never said "Good morning", anything. I actually thought he was an impostor, and I told him so.

You'd go to try to see him and he'd disappear. You'd knock on the door and he'd run out the back. You'd go into his room and he'd put a golf club in your hand, he had this little putting thing on the office floor and you'd have to try and putt!

It was a tactic. By the time you'd done all that you'd calmed down and forgotten what you'd gone in there for!

Not surprisingly I went on the transfer list. I don't know if they wouldn't sell me or if no-one came in for me, but I was scoring quite a lot of goals for the reserves and was still playing in the youth team as well at that time. I was still only 19. But then everything changed.

In 1965/66 the first team struggled to keep their heads above water. They won just one game between October and February and hit rock bottom after Christmas. If you look back through history, the team had picked itself for ages: Macedo, Cohen, Langley, Mullery, Dodgin, Lowe. That defence never changed! Then up front it was Leggat and whoever else.

After such a bad run, Vic thought we were going to go down. So he drafted in a load of young kids – me, Les Barrett, Brian Nichols and Freddie Callaghan – and dropped the old-timers who'd been there for years. Another youngster was John Dempsey, the Irish centre-half. John came in at the back alongside Brian Nichols. Like me, these lads had come up through the youth team, so as far as I was concerned the more of us lads that got in the first team the better. We knew each other, worked for each other, but we didn't really have anything in common with the older guys.

Then he bought Mark "Pancho" Pearson from Manchester United, who was an experienced player when he came to us. He'd earned his nickname because of the Mexican look his sideburns gave him. Pancho was good for a season or so. He could slow the game down, didn't run around a lot and if anybody went and tackled him they didn't want to do it again!

Pancho knew all the tricks in the book. In the match which ended that horrendous run at the end of February against league leaders Liverpool at the Cottage, I scored both goals in a 2-0 win. One of the goals was controversial as Bill Shankly claimed I'd handled. Okay, I'll admit it now – it was what the basketball guys over here call a "double dribble"! But all that was overshadowed when Pancho suckered Ian St John. Mark fell over and the referee decided St John had hit or headbutted him. Saint was on his way off the pitch – and we were on our way off the bottom of the table…

I was back in the first team, with a 35 per cent pay increase! It would be almost the last time I enjoyed a pay rise. That was the season that we avoided relegation at Northampton, and I scored a hat-trick – the game I've chosen as the Match of My Life. In case you wonder why I didn't pick our 8-1 win at Halifax in 1969 where I scored five, all I can say is this – my main memory of that game is that with 20 minutes to go Bill Dodgin, the then manager, told me to stop playing and go out on the right wing. So I could have scored a couple more!

While the events of that night at the Shay were unexpected, the Northampton game was always going to be a tester. For a start, we'd lost 4-0 at home to Leicester the previous game, which was very depressing. But in fact our fortunes were on the up, and had been ever since Vic Buckingham brought in Dave Sexton, who'd not long been sacked by Leyton Orient. Dave and Bill Taylor were the best coaches I played under at Fulham. They got us organised, told us to play, gave us some confidence and we started winning games. When you start winning confidence grows and breeds more success.

Dave did so well at Fulham that his next stop was Highbury. It had been his idea to bring the young guys in, and the history books remind me we'd won seven of the nine games that led up to the County Ground showdown in April '66.

The only trouble was Northampton had started winning too! If you look at the record of the last 15 games or so, every time we won they won! They'd climbed the divisions, from fourth to first, in just four seasons under the former Welsh international Dave Bowen. They'd found the step up to the top flight tough at first, but then their form picked up after February and the Cobblers had lost just once in ten games. They were nobody's pushovers – even though, like Swansea the following decade, they'd eventually sink just as quickly. Things really came to a head when we played each other as there were only three games remaining after that. The question of who would go down with Blackburn was effectively to be decided on that one game.

I partnered many strikers up front for Fulham over the years, but the first and best was without a doubt Graham Leggat. He liked to play off a big striker because he wasn't very big himself, but he was brave as a lion, quick and aggressive. That said, playing the two of us together was very much of a muchness. I preferred to play with someone like Vic Halom, a big guy who'd go for all the high balls and I'd pick up the pieces. I didn't think I won too many headers, but I scored quite a few near-posters coming in for crosses and darting in front of the defender. I didn't score much at the far post or in the air. I used to follow the big guys round and pick up chances off them; it made my job easier.

Graham was also very good out wide, which was just as well. Vic Buckingham signed Allan Clarke from Walsall that spring to bolster our fight against relegation. But Allan couldn't get in the team as our form picked up so well. Eventually, though, it became clear that one of either Graham or I would have to drop back to accommodate him. So for a few games I played on the right wing.

Clarkie was a good player, a very good player – the best natural finisher I ever played with. He was the first of umpteen different people Fulham tried to replace me with over the years: Frank Large, Vic Halom, Joe Gilroy... Some of the others basically weren't good enough, so I'd always get back in. What upset me, though, was that I'd still be on the same money and they were paying all these new guys big bucks. Me and Les Barrett, all the ones who'd been there many years, never seemed to get a pay rise!

Running the show in midfield, of course, was the one and only Johnny Haynes. He was a hard taskmaster. He used to whip these balls out to you, and your heart would start bubbling a little bit worrying about the tongue lashing I might get if you mis-controlled it – remember I was only an 18-year-old at the time!

I used to run inside for George Cohen to steam down the wing and smash crosses in. When they came to the near post I'd redirect them with flicks and stuff, and scored quite a lot of goals doing that. If you scored goals, you stayed in the team! The first goal I got against Northampton was created like that – a cross from George to the near post – and the second was from a cross from Graham Leggat, so he must have been playing wide: we were fairly flexible in that way. He'd go out wide or I'd go out wide depending on the situation.

I remember there was a great atmosphere that day. On one side the County Ground was open, because there was a cricket field there [the football club shared their home at the County Ground with Northamptonshire County Cricket Club]. People were even standing along that side. There were nearly 25,000 there, which is a record that will stand forever now they play at Sixfields. Northampton came out like gangbusters, it was a real crash-helmet job to start with. They got in front when our keeper Jack McLelland palmed the ball to their centre-forward, George Hudson, and they could have scored two or three more as they piled the pressure on.

Jack, a very athletic keeper on his day, was saved on this particular day by Bobby Robson, Robbo equalised with a great 25-yarder, swapping passes with Pearson before belting it home. But then Bobby went from hero to villain when his poor clearing header set up Kiernan for Northampton's second.

That was when we had a real stroke of luck. It was obviously destiny when the linesman slipped and didn't see McLelland scoop Hudson's shot, which had come down from the crossbar, back from behind the goal-line. At least we only went in 2-1 down...

I don't recall any stirring half-time speech, and I wouldn't have expected any of the senior players to have rallied the troops. You didn't get a lot of comments from the older men because they kept themselves to themselves. It was all about self-preservation, survival of the fittest – that's how it is in the pro game. If Vic Buckingham did any pre-match and half-time talks, I can't remember one!

After I touched in that George Cohen cross on 65 minutes for our second goal, I think we would have settled for a draw, having twice come back from a goal down. That big centre-forward, Hudson, was causing us a lot of problems. He was good in the air and our defence wasn't, to be blunt. When you see the final score of 4-2 it looks quite comfortable, but I can assure you it really wasn't.

Five minutes before the end, our full-back Brian Nichols kicked Walden's goal-bound header off the line. So it was a relief to get back up to the other end of the pitch.

Then the third goal, and my second, came with just two minutes left as I headed in a Graham Leggat cross. We were ahead for the first time. There was just enough time left for Northampton to throw everything forward and, as so often happens, we caught them on the break. With 19 players in the Fulham box, left-back Brian Nichols lumped it out to me. I was in the centre circle and had a clean run-through. It was me and Graham Leggat against the goalkeeper, Norman Coe. I was thinking of rolling it square for Graham, but the keeper made my decision for me. He came flying right out to the edge of the box so I just went round him and put it in.

Unlike that vital win over Liverpool, no-one was dismissed at Northampton and there were no handball goals. We won it fair and square, eleven on eleven – and, to make things better, much to our fans' delight, Chelsea were losing their FA Cup semi-final to Sheffield Wednesday up the road at Villa Park. Winning such a crucial game was a breath of fresh air to us. I know the over-riding emotion was relief that we'd got through it, but I really can't remember too much more. The crowd was on the field, as Ken Coton's famous pics show, and there was an electric atmosphere that you didn't get often in those days.

Having retained our top-flight status by the skin of our teeth, we stayed up for another couple of seasons. But it was always a struggle, and we were increasingly relying on the youth players to keep us up. When I was on the ground staff there were 15 lads and I think ten of them signed pro which is a phenomenal record. Marshy was one of them, Fred, Brian, Terry Parmenter. They may not all have had long careers, but many of them made it to the first team, which again you don't see much these days.

Fulham was a different club from any other. It was a great place, full of characters, but some of the training we did was basic: two warm-up laps and a five-a-side. For me, as a young player, I did my learning on the pitch, watching the first team. If the first team were playing five-a-sides and they were short, I'd get called in and that's how I learned to play. Today everything's so coached and I don't know if that's good or bad. You couldn't help but learn when you watched players like Johnny Haynes, Alan Mullery and George Cohen. You picked this up and that up. These days it's all about athletic ability.

When Bobby Robson became manager, I got on all right with him. He was new, it was his first job, and I think he had a difficult task trying to coach players he'd played with. He obviously knew what he was doing, but he needed to do it with people who didn't know him. It's hard to get out the big stick with people you've been playing with for ten years. It's also hard to get a response from certain players. I remember him coming up to me and saying "How do I get Les Barrett to do this?" and I said "I ain't worried about Les Barrett, I'm worried about me"!

In all honesty, the players looked after themselves; whoever the coach was didn't make that much of a difference. I had a great rapport with Bill Taylor, as well as Dave Sexton. Bill Dodgin was good too. But managers like Alec Stock and Vic Buckingham were more characters than coaches.

After a decade in the first-team picture I decided to move on in late 1973. No-one outside the club really knows this, but the fact was that I had been supposed to be going to Chelsea for the previous four years! After Dave Sexton left us he went to Arsenal, and he tried to get me and John Dempsey to follow him. The Fulham board wouldn't let us go. Then Dave went to Chelsea and Fulham definitely wouldn't let me go there. Then, when Leicester came in for me, Alec Stock took me into his office and told me they needed money to pay for the Riverside Stand, which was under construction. So they sold me and Paul Went, me for £70,000 and Went to Portsmouth for £150,000. This was on a Tuesday, and Alec said "If you wait till Friday Dave Sexton will be back off holiday and I can flog you to Chelsea for 20 grand more." I said "No thanks, I've been waiting four years for this – I'm off to Leicester!"

Fulham had been bringing in older players like Cliffie Jones and Terry Dyson on free transfers and giving them big signing-on bonuses. The rest of us were on £50 a week; left behind again! I was due a testimonial and negotiated one for a guaranteed ten grand. But they only let me have it a year after I left, so there was only about 1,800 people there. It was no way to end my love-hate relationship with the Cottage fans.

In those days the fans wouldn't put up with what they do today – playing it across the back, putting it back to the goalkeeper. They wanted it put in the opposition box, they liked big centre-forwards who went smashing in, bashing into goalkeepers, that sort of thing. Well, that wasn't me. Jimmy Conway, Les Barrett and myself were the opposite; we relied on our pace and our quick feet.

When it worked it worked, when it didn't they'd give you all sorts of abuse. But if you scored goals they loved you!

After four years at Filbert Street, I came to Tulsa, where I still live, and played here for the Roughnecks for a couple of years. Then I got into coaching. When the North American Soccer League folded in 1984, we decided to wait and get our kids through high school. Then I got into the insurance business and I've been doing that ever since.

I coach at Tulsa Soccer Club with Keith Eddy, who used to play for Sheffield United and Watford. He runs the club; I coach the two older boys' teams. There are boys' and girls' teams all the way from Under-8 to Under-18s. The kids over here get far more opportunity than they do in England. There are lots of kids at youth level playing soccer. We're going to a tournament soon at a town just outside Dallas where there'll be 350 teams of different age groups. You can imagine the financial impact for all the shops, hotels, etc, of all those teams and their families going there. What I do now is try to help kids get soccer scholarships at college by taking them to showcases where the colleges will come and look at them.

When Fulham's Brian McBride started over here I got wind of him and from what I heard I felt he'd go far, but I think he should have gone to Europe eight years earlier than he did. He's the kind of player I felt would do well in the English game. He has done well, don't get me wrong, but I think he'd have done better going over to the UK younger. We had a kid here I worked with, Joe-Max Moore, who went to Everton. I coached him a little bit; his dad used to own the NASL team I played for. Joe-Max went off to California, graduated to Germany and then to England.

We've got a 14-year-old kid at our club now I'd love to see come over, but it's difficult for Americans unless they've got British parentage – they have to get visas and work permits etc. At 14 you have to get a student visa as well. He's got talent, but if he stays over here any longer he'll be off to college and, in my opinion, that's not the way to go.

Leicester have a very active former players' network, but I haven't seen too many of my Fulham colleagues for years. The exception is Johnny Haynes, and my meeting with him came about more or less by chance. When I was last in Britain in early 2005, I decided to see a cousin I hadn't seen since I was a boy; she was my dad's sister's daughter. I knew Haynesy was living in Edinburgh, where my cousin also lived, and I called him out of the blue. I hadn't seen him since '68 and he said it'd be nice to see me. I had a great time, and it was completely different from what I remembered. He made me feel really welcome.

What I admire about Johnny is that he hasn't taken anything out of the game, even though he's had opportunities to make money. I asked him why he hasn't become a TV pundit, like so many players have. For some of them, the longer they stop playing the better they get! Some of them weren't that good, but he was good. And he said he'd simply never wanted to.

When I was talking to Johnny, we worked out that I'd scored a hundred and odd goals for Fulham, yet there was only one season when we were anywhere near the top. We were always down the bottom and I said "What if I'd played for a team that was up the top, how many goals would I have scored then?" But when you're young you just want to play.

You won't believe this, but I've never ever seen myself play on TV. I don't really want to. Dennis Rofe called me the other day and said he'd got a DVD of when I was at Leicester and I was on there a few times scoring goals. He wanted to send it to me, so maybe I'll watch it once and probably never look at it again. It feels like it's a different lifetime.

Football didn't have the superstar quality it does now. I enjoyed it, but treated it like a job. If I'd thought about the pressure, I'd have gone crazy! I had fun, though, and I wish I could do it again.

JOHN MITCHELL
FORWARD 1972–1978

BORN   12th March 1952, St. Albans
SIGNED   February 1972 from St. Albans City; £3,000
FULHAM CAREER   194 games, 60 goals
HONOURS   FA Cup Runners-up Medal 1975
LEFT   Transferred to Millwall, June 1978; £100,000
(New Millwall club record)

Signed from non-League, 'Mitch' fired Fulham to their first ever Wembley appearance with his semi-final goals. His late winner even provoked the famously lugubrious Bobby Moore to run the length of the Maine Road pitch to embrace him. Injury-prone, but with the heart of a lion, Mitch was a memorable leader of the line and in many fans' view was never adequately replaced.

Fulham 1 v Birmingham City 1

FA Cup Semi-final
Saturday 5th April 1975

Hillsborough
Attendance 55,000

After a replay Fulham win through to their first ever FA Cup Final and their first appearance in any major final

Teams

Peter Mellor	1	Peter Latchford
John Fraser	2	Malcolm Page
Les Strong	3	Gary Pendrey
Alan Mullery	4	Howard Kendall
John Lacy	5	Joe Gallagher
Bobby Moore	6	John Roberts
John Mitchell	7	Alan Campbell
Jimmy Conway	8	Trevor Francis
(Sub. John Dowie)		
Viv Busby	9	Kenny Burns
Alan Slough	10	Bob Hatton
Les Barrett	11	Gordon Taylor

Mitchell 65	**Scorers**	Gallagher 58

Referee: W Gow

Fulham 1 v Birmingham City 0

After extra time

FA Cup Semi-final replay
Wednesday 9th April 1975

Maine Road
Attendance 35,025

Teams

Peter Mellor	1	Peter Latchford
John Fraser	2	Malcolm Page
Les Strong	3	Steve Bryant
Alan Mullery	4	Howard Kendall
John Lacy	5	Joe Gallagher
Bobby Moore	6	Gary Pendrey
John Mitchell	7	Paul Hendrie
John Dowie	8	Trevor Francis
Viv Busby	9	Kenny Burns
Alan Slough	10	Bob Hatton
Les Barrett	11	Gordon Taylor

Mitchell 120	**Scorers**	

Referee: Mr W Gow

As MOST OLDER Fulham supporters will remember, my career was, to an extent, blighted by injury. In my first season, I notched up 36 Division Two appearances, and scored 11 goals, but in the next campaign I featured only 13 times. My injuries were many and varied but, apart from a bad back injury and pelvic problems, it was ankle injuries which caused many of the difficulties and kept me out of the game for fairly long periods. I think quite a few people saw me as a brave centre-forward. Equally, others perhaps saw me as a stupid centre-forward because I sustained so many injuries. As far as I was concerned, I had to go in where it hurts, and that probably dictated the amount of injuries I received. Anyway, I always seemed to be coming back from one injury or another, and when you return to the side after a break, it usually takes a game or two to regain match fitness and, in my case, to start scoring goals again. Looking back, I think I was probably a better player than I thought I was at the time, because my career at Fulham was so stop-start. I hope I was, anyway.

Injuries will always be a problem in football, but in my day, pitches always seemed to be either very bumpy, or very muddy. There are some great players in today's Premiership, and some very good ones in the lower divisions, but they do now mostly play on beautifully prepared pitches – and they don't get tackled from behind. At least, not very often. There has, of course, also been a revolution in the treatment of injuries in the last few years, and much greater attention is paid to diet and nutrition.

It was an ankle injury which caused me to retire as a player at the age of 28. I was with Millwall by this time and the damage was done during a training session. It was nobody's fault, just one of those things. At that time, players tended to carry injuries and many of us actually played on when we shouldn't have done. Thanks to the wonderful invention of the cortisone injection. In my case, when I finished playing, I had quite a severe limp following several operations and it was only after I retired and booked myself in for one more operation that I was able to walk normally again. Even so, I still have to be protective of that left leg, and I can't do too much at any one time. Thankfully, I can play a round of golf, which for me is essential, but I do start to limp a bit at the end of the round, in particular during the winter months.

The game I've chosen as the Match of My Life actually turned into two games – the FA Cup semi-final and semi-final replay against Birmingham City in 1975. I had, as ever, missed quite a few games that season. Viv Busby and Alan Mullery were the main goalscorers in the League, and I didn't get my name on the scoresheet until March. I bagged one at Bristol Rovers, and then scored both our goals in a 2-1 victory at Norwich City on Bank Holiday Monday that effectively cost the Canaries their chance of promotion that season.

As the end of the 1974-75 season approached, we were in a mid-table position in Division Two, but we had enjoyed a most extraordinary run in the FA Cup. In those days, drawn Cup games were always replayed, no matter how many games it took. We met Second Division Hull City in the Third Round, and beat them 1-0 on a neutral ground – Leicester City's Filbert Street – at the third attempt, with an Alan Slough goal. We then went one better against another club from our own division, Brian Clough's Nottingham Forest, and took four games to dispose of them, finally winning 2-1 at Nottingham with a brace from Viv Busby. I was in and out of the side at this stage, and I did not feature in the remarkable 2-1 victory at First Division leaders Everton in the Fifth Round (again, two goals from Viv) nor in the 1-0 win at Carlisle in Round Six – where goalkeeper Peter Mellor played a blinder, and Les Barrett scored our winner. Looking back, it appears as if I was saving myself for the semis, in which I was to score the goals that took us to Wembley!

In those semi-finals, we were the only side from outside the top flight. West Ham faced Ipswich, while we were drawn against Birmingham City. The Blues were struggling somewhat in the First Division at the time, and were not totally clear of the relegation zone, although in the event they did avoid the drop, and Luton, Chelsea and Carlisle went down. For some reason, I expect all Fulham fans were quite pleased to note the identity of one of those sides!

Naturally, I remember all my team-mates very well. Goalkeeper Peter Mellor was a big lad, with a very dominant presence. He should be revered as the man who got us to Wembley, having made a number of outstanding saves throughout the competition – especially some great ones at Carlisle. Sadly, in many people's eyes he is now better remembered for the goals he conceded in the Final. Such is the lot of a goalkeeper.

The defence was a mixture of youth and experience, with the accent on youth. John Fraser was one of the nicest guys you could have in the dressing room, he was a very steady player, and an unsung hero. You knew what you were going to get with John. He never over-elaborated. Every good side needs a player like him. As for Les Strong – I think it's all been said already. Any further insults from me would be superfluous. He was, and is, a one-off. He's also a great lad and it was a terrible shame when he missed the Final through injury. He made light of it, and to an extent he is still making light of it, but I know deep down he was very upset at the time, as indeed we all were.

John Lacy, nicknamed Blakey, because we thought he looked like Blakey from the TV series *On The Buses,* was a tall centre-half with a B.Sc. in Economics. Because of his studies, he came into the game quite late in life. He wasn't the swiftest in the business and, like many of us in that team, he was a good, rather than a great player. He eventually went on to bigger things at Tottenham, and this was something he deserved. Blakey was a great guy, and very funny, and he combined very well with Bobby Moore – his height making him much better in the air than his more illustrious partner.

As for Bobby himself, what can one say? He could hardly run, couldn't turn, couldn't head a ball, and had absolutely no left foot. But he was the world's greatest defender. He had a better head on his shoulders than any of the others, and even though he was coming towards the end of his career when he joined Fulham, he was still a great player and a tremendous asset to the side. I remember his first ever pass to me. It was very hard, and about three yards to my right, so I had to turn sharply to reach it. I thought: He only passed the ball 15 yards, so why didn't he pass it to my feet? But as I turned, the player marking me was on my left side – so in fact Bobby had beaten him for me. That was the difference. It was a tragedy that he was shunned by the FA after he retired. Bobby Moore was the nicest person I ever met in football and could have contributed enormously to the game at a time when it was most needed.

Alan Mullery was another great player. Mullers was very different to Bobby in the dressing room. To some he seemed a lot less warm, and yet he was an inspirational captain who, together with manager Alec Stock, was able to convince us all that we were good enough to get to Wembley. Mullers always concentrated very hard on his game, and I think, apart from his great natural ability, that was what made him such a great player.

Like most of the squad, he could also be very funny when the mood took him. Often, just before a game, he would pull his shorts up to just under his arms and say something like: "Come on lads. Let's take 'em." It was not a pretty sight.

Scotsman John Dowie was another of our unsung heroes. He was great on the ball and a very hard worker, and he was to play a significant part in getting us to those Twin Towers. Sadly for him, like Strongy, he was not to feature in the Final. He wasn't injured, and it must have been a hard decision for Alec Stock to take to leave him out in favour of Jimmy Conway after the contribution John had made to Fulham's cause.

I used to travel up to games from Hertfordshire with two other members of our strike force, Viv Busby and Alan Slough, so we were pretty close and had a lot of fun together. Buzza was a hot and cold player. When he was hot, there was nobody to touch him. He probably should have scored more goals than he did, but he certainly did score some vital ones, including of course the two in the fourth game against Nottingham Forest, and another brace in the Fifth Round at Goodison Park – a game nobody expected Fulham to win. In my view, Alan Slough was the most underrated of the lot. He was an exceptional player, who would definitely make it in the modern game. He could score goals, he defended well and he was another really genuinely nice person.

Then there was "Boo Boo" Barrett, a very talented and speedy winger who I believe could have gone right to the top in different circumstances. He was quite shy and perhaps not really aware of just how good he was – I understand he turned down the chance to join Manchester United at one stage. You may wonder how Les got his nickname. Although he was a marvellous winger, he did occasionally appear to nod off when nothing much was happening – even during a game. On one occasion, someone ran up behind him and said "Boo!" and Les jumped half out of his skin.

Jimmy Conway was also a speedy winger, who gained international recognition with the Republic of Ireland. Jim had 16 brothers and sisters, and one of the brothers – John – also played for Fulham. Jim played in the first game against Birmingham, but not in the replay, and although he was to play in the Final I don't think he was fully fit.

I have got very good memories of the first semi-final game. At first, I wasn't certain that I'd be selected to play, but once I knew I was definitely in the side, I felt great. I woke up in the morning knowing I was going to score. Footballers have feelings like that sometimes. I was in the middle of a good run too, so I went into the game full of confidence.

There was a marvellous atmosphere at Hillsborough, which was hardly surprising with a gate of 55,000. Our fans seemed to believe that little old Second Division Fulham were really going to Wembley this time, and that spurred us all on. The first half was goalless, but we more than held our own. With Les Barrett turning Malcolm Page inside out with his speedy runs, our forwards were generally getting the better of the Birmingham defence, and I was giving Blues central defender Joe Gallagher, in particular, the run around.

Then, five minutes into the second period, the ball was knocked from Mullers to Sloughie, who touched it on to me. I wasn't known for always having the greatest first touch, and on this occasion the ball bobbled a bit, but one thing I could do was to shoot with either foot. As soon as I hit it – on the volley, with my left foot – I knew it was a goal all the way. It was an emotional moment after all those injuries, so I headed towards the fans, who had always been great to me, even during the bad times. I then found I had ten players on top of me, and I was lucky not to be injured yet again!

We had other clear-cut chances, including a shot from Viv Busby which was deflected off Dave Latchford's leg, and we felt we should have finished the game off. On the day, we were by far the better side. The former Arsenal defender, John Roberts, was marking me, and he got dropped for the second game. Of course, things were rather spoilt for us when Birmingham equalized courtesy of Joe Gallagher, their central defender. We would have to do it all again, but with Alec Stock and Mullers to encourage us, we knew we could beat them. My goal had been described as a "superb dipping volley" and I was sure I could put in a repeat performance.

Incidentally, I met Joe Gallagher again in 2005 at a function in Birmingham. He was the guest – and I was a plant, sitting in the dark at the back of the audience. They were talking about the first game, my goal and his, and about the replay. When it came to question time, I stood up, and in my best Brummie accent said: "But Joe, you were very slow on the day. That John Mitchell was too quick for you". I kept coming back to him, telling him he was slow on the day, and that he couldn't cope with that John Mitchell. After the third time, the MC revealed who I was. He introduced me as "the man who broke our hearts in 1975" and I had to stand up in front of loads of Birmingham fans. You can imagine the reception I got. I'm lucky to be alive, really.

I'm not saying that we expected yet one more replay, but in the circumstances it was perhaps not all that surprising when we earned ourselves one. As it happens the West Ham versus Ipswich game also went to a replay and it was the first time a double deadlock had occurred in the two FA Cup semi-finals for 23 years. We got a lot of media attention after that game at Hillsborough. This was inevitable, given that we were in the Second Division, and had comedian Tommy Trinder as our chairman. It seemed that Tommy's catch phrase "You lucky people" might at last apply to Fulham supporters. I had picked up a slight groin strain (inevitably) and thought at first I might not make the replay. But in the end all was well, and I took to the field in an almost unchanged side.

It was a very cold night in Manchester. A lot of fans had travelled up from London, and we were determined to do it for them. We knew Birmingham were not likely to play that badly again, but we also knew we had a good defence and that a Cup Final appearance was within our grasp.

I was right. The Blues didn't play that badly again. I think their manager Fred Goodwin had stirred them up a bit about being in a semi-final against a Second Division team. But we gave a good as we got in a scrappy, bitty game.

It wasn't a great match to watch, I'm sure, with Birmingham generally playing more defensively than they had in the first game. At one stage Joe Gallagher lost control of the ball and let in Viv Busby, whose shot hit the outside of a post, but there weren't too many scoring chances for either side.

As the game rolled on, it became clear that one goal would probably be enough to settle it. Towards the end, it was obvious Birmingham were running out of steam. They'd given it their best shot, but they hadn't broken us down. The game went into extra time, and it began to seem that we would be in for a second replay, this time at Highbury (I think we had already played more matches in one campaign than any other team in the history of the competition). Then, no more than a few seconds before the end of extra time, we mounted an attack and Alan Slough put the ball across. It came towards me, but I knew it was way too high. I didn't know who was behind me, but I thought that if Les Barrett or John Dowie were there, they might get to it and head it either at, or across, the goal; so I readied myself for the knockback.

In the event, John nodded it across goal and I just got my foot around the defender, Joe Gallagher. The ball struck keeper Dave Latchford, then it rebounded off my chest and knee as I lunged forward. At least, I think that's what happened – after all, it is more than thirty years ago! I definitely remember being on the ground on my hands and knees, trying to get up, looking at the ball rolling towards the goal, and I honestly thought it wasn't going to cross the line. But it did, and the Fulham fans behind that goal went berserk. So did most of the players. Those that had the energy anyway. Even Bobby Moore danced down the pitch to give me an enormous hug! With so little time left, we all knew that, somehow, we'd done it – and we would soon be walking down Wembley Way.

Bobby Moore and I had to do a live interview for the BBC's Sportsnight after that, and the television people kept us hanging around. We were wet and very cold, and Bobby very nearly walked away from it. But we did the interview, and then had a great night – I seem to recall that there was a great deal of champagne about. One newspaper claimed that there were 80 bottles of it, but I think that may be a slight exaggeration – at least that's my story! All I can really remember is that at 6 am we were still up and still celebrating. We then walked out into Piccadilly Square in Manchester and bought all the papers. After all, we had to make sure we'd won – and I had to make sure I'd scored! The papers were full of praise for us. Tommy Trinder was quoted as saying that it would be the first time he had been to Wembley and not had a seat behind a pillar, while Alec Stock recalled that, before I scored, he had been shouting to the defenders; "Remember we're at Highbury on Monday."

Under the headline "Mitch, you're magnificent" David Miller wrote in the *Daily Express*:

John Mitchell last night shot himself into FA Cup history and Fulham into their first final. He did it with an unforgettable goal just twelve seconds from the end of extra time in the semi-final replay at Maine Road. This was a moment I shall treasure throughout the rest of my time watching this unpredictable game of football, for if ever a team had looked beaten for most of the first hour, it was Fulham. Yet at the end of eighteen and a half hours of FA Cup battle and eleven matches, Fulham's Cockney pride and courage, so nearly drowned by revitalised Birmingham in that first hour, surged once more to the front.

The spirit, the refusal to lie down which has carried them through ties in Hull, Leicester, Nottingham (twice), Everton, Carlisle and Sheffield was now epitomised by Mitchell's last-gasp goal as the Second Division Londoners hurled themselves back into a game that had seemed lost...

I wouldn't quite agree that we looked a beaten side for most of the first hour, but even so, that's a nice piece of writing, and Mr Miller certainly captured the spirit of the occasion and the spirit of our Fulham side.

Naturally, the Final against West Ham proved to be a disappointment. This is Fulham after all. We had come so far, only to fall at the last hurdle. It was a wonderful day, though, and I'll never forget walking out at Wembley. The Cup campaign may have ended in disappointment but, ironically, I was about to enjoy my most successful period with Fulham.

The following season, 1975/76, made me look at football in a different way. In a stroke of genius, Fulham signed George Best and Rodney Marsh early in the campaign. When I heard about this, I can remember driving to the ground thinking: We've already got four forwards, now they've signed two more. Am I going to get into the side? So, in a way I was disappointed, but after the first training session with them I felt more inspired than frustrated. George was the most physically balanced player I'd ever seen. Rodney was a big fellow (I don't think people realised just how big he was) and he would simply sway past people. Best and Marshy were, in a sense, coming back to prove a point, but they were very jovial about it all and they wanted to enjoy themselves.

My normal role in the pre-match kick-abouts was to test the keeper, but with George and Rodney there it became a competition about who could hit the crossbar the most times. The games themselves were pure showbiz. Gates doubled overnight, and even if the results had been atrocious, I don't think it would have mattered. Actually, if you look at the record, they weren't all that good. But we did have a lot of fun!

The wonderful thing was that there was great camaraderie amongst the players. This had been with us during the cup run, and it was still there. Now, six or seven of us would go to a restaurant called the Starlight in Fulham Palace Road. Mooro and George in particular loved it, because they could sit in a corner of the restaurant, and no-one bothered us. They could be themselves. Les Strong and I would take the mickey out of the "stars" and they loved it all. The banter was marvellous, and it was a very special time. As things turned out, I remained injury free and played in 38 of the 42 League games that season. I netted 21 times in all competitions, and scored four in a 6-1 win over Orient at the end of the campaign, all Fulham's goals coming in a remarkable first half.

I was less prolific during 1977/78, although I did play in most of the Division Two games. Bobby Campbell had taken over as manager from Alec Stock during the previous season, and other changes were afoot. I had the utmost respect for Alec Stock. He was a wonderful man and I know he is remembered with great affection by all who knew him. The chairman also changed, as did the board, and Fulham became a different club. In 1976/77, while all this was going on, I'd qualified for a free holiday by scoring more than twenty goals during that campaign. The holiday turned out to be a fortnight at new owner Ernie Clay's hotel, while the hotel itself turned out to be full of refugees. I also had to pay my own fare to get there. Not really the way to treat your top goalscorer!

I enjoyed a marvellous time at Fulham, and I've never had any regrets about the years I spent at the club. How could I regret playing for a club which, on my twenty-first birthday, gave me the chance to play against Santos – and to nutmeg the legendary Pele? The club, the players, and the supporters gave me many happy memories, but things had changed and now it was time to move on. I was 25 and needed a fresh challenge.

I was sold to Millwall for, at the time, a record fee of £100,000, but soon afterwards sustained that bad ankle injury, and from then on I was always struggling. For a long time I had injections before every game to deaden the pain, something that would not happen now. There was a very different atmosphere at Millwall. It was more intense, but it was still a very good, professional one. I liked the manager George Petchey, who was doing a very good job with limited resources, and I was disappointed that I couldn't do more to help out at the Den. It seemed I had been there no time at all when I was forced to retire.

I'm still involved with football, but I no longer make my living at it. After I stopped playing I managed – and later owned – St. Albans City. I was a sort of Mohamed Al Fayed, really. Well, perhaps not. While I was managing there we won promotion three times, and should then have gone into the Conference league, but we weren't allowed in because we had a tree on the terrace behind one goal. It was a good stadium, where England trained, but at the time there was a lot of politics involved with promotion to the Conference; it didn't happen as of right as it does today with the new structure in place in the non-league game. I'm afraid it killed my enthusiasm and motivation and I decided to pass the reins on to someone who had the energy to take the club on. I got out of football completely for a time.

I couldn't stay out forever though, and now I'm a director of Luton Town. I suppose that makes me a sort of Eric Morecambe! Actually, I've been a director there twice. The first time, it was not a happy experience, but now it's very different. There are four of us who took the club out of receivership a couple of years ago. We've cut costs, have a policy of bringing on young players, coupled with an excellent scouting system, and have a very good young manager in Mike Newell. Last year, 2004/05, we won the League One Championship by 12 points. Early this season, we beat two of the sides which came down from the Premiership (Crystal Palace away, and then Southampton at home) and we currently have a very good young team. Naturally, we have our sights set on even greater things, including a move to a brand new stadium. Perhaps we'll one day meet Fulham in the Premiership – or perhaps at Wembley. I'd love to think so.

LES STRONG
FULL-BACK 1971—1983

BORN   3rd July 1953, Streatham
SIGNED   June 1971 from Apprentice
FULHAM CAREER   427 games, 6 goals
HONOURS   Promotion from Division Three 1981-82
LEFT   Free transfer to Crystal Palace, August 1983

Les is one of Fulham's great characters. Coach Bill Taylor regarded him as "our joker in the pack." But it was his often overlooked playing skills that earned him a decade as a first-team player. As captain of the side from 1977 to 1982, he led his team to promotion back to the Second Division. But the one thing he will always be remembered for is missing the 1975 FA Cup Final, the biggest day of his career, through injury. Most players who suffer such indignation would refuse to talk about it. Les is different.

Fulham 0 v West Ham United 2

FA Cup Final
Saturday 3 May 1975

Wembley Stadium
Attendance 100,000

Fulham come off second best in their first ever Wembley Final

Teams

Peter Mellor	1	Mervyn Day
John Cutbush	2	John McDowell
John Fraser	3	Frank Lampard
Alan Mullery	4	Billy Bonds
John Lacy	5	Tommy Taylor
Bobby Moore	6	Kevin Lock
John Mitchell	7	Bill Jennings
Jimmy Conway	8	Graham Paddon
Viv Busby	9	Alan Taylor
Alan Slough	10	Trevor Brooking
Les Barrett	11	Pat Holland

Scorers   Alan Taylor 60, 64

Referee: P Partridge

"LES STRONG? Didn't you miss the Cup Final?" It's funny. I played ten seasons for Fulham, made over 400 appearances and was even captain. But it's a safe bet that it's the first thing Fulham supporters say when they meet me. It's what I'm remembered for, even now, thirty years later. And the first thing I say? "Don't mention the bloody Cup Final!"

Of all the games to miss through injury, it's ironic it was that one. I hardly ever got injured in my career. In the nine years I played after 1975, I think I missed about 13 games in all. That's about a game and a half each season – and some of those were suspensions! I was 21 that year. I'd got into the side about halfway through the season before and in the Cup Final season, 1974/75, I played in every single game until the injury came – and with that record Cup run of 11 games, there were a lot of them!

It was two weeks before Wembley. Our penultimate home game, against Portsmouth. Me and George Graham went for the same ball, he shoulder-charged me and my studs got caught in the ground. It wasn't a bad tackle or anything, but I managed to tear my knee ligaments. I was having a good season, too. It was the year I really established myself in the side and we were playing some decent foot-ball. Maybe not quite enough for promotion – I think we were one or two players short for that. We eventually finished ninth that year. You criticise players at the time, but in hindsight we had a good team. Players like Les Barrett and Jimmy Conway used to get stick for being so-called "home" players – they'd disappear on a wet January night at Oldham. But play them at the Cottage and they were fantastic – great entertainment. But as I said, we were just a couple of squad players short. If someone got injured we just didn't have the cover.

At the time the Cup run started in January, we were loitering around mid-table. It looked like being just another season. The odds on us seeing Wembley were something like 500-1 so we certainly didn't have any notions about going all the way. At the time, Hull at home in the Third Round was just a nothing game. Little did we know that we were about to embark on the longest ever Cup run in football history.

That first Hull game set the tone. We went one nil up through Jimmy Conway and then Hull equalised. We never came from behind during that Cup run. It was always us throwing away leads. And we never won at home either – talk about making life hard for ourselves! The replay up in Hull was about three days later, and that was 2-2. But this was in the era before penalties, so we had a second replay at Filbert Street another few days after that. We beat them 1-0 – Alan Slough. It was a real non-event though. Both sets of fans had to travel a long way to see these two sides slog it out against each other for the third time in just over a week. So as you can imagine, not many bothered. We just wanted to get the game out of the way. Ironically enough we played Hull again on 1st February in the League – as if playing them three times in nine days in January wasn't enough!

And if only we'd known what lay ahead in the Fourth Round against Forest! It took us four attempts to get past them! Forest had a really tricky winger who I had to mark – an Irish feller whose name I can't remember [Miah Dennehy]. I got substituted in the first game which was a thrilling 0-0 draw at home. I was having a shocker – that winger was giving me a lot of trouble so our manager, Alec Stock, pulled me off. But he put me back in for the next game, the replay up at the City Ground. I was delighted to be back in, but I had to do everything to keep that winger under control. He's what I really remember about that round. I never really had much trouble with wingers in my career. Only about half a dozen in all gave me any real problems, and they were all the same – short and fast, and he was one of them. So all I really cared about was keeping him under control and not getting yanked off!

I don't know why we didn't play at a neutral ground in the Fourth Round second and third replays. All I remember is that there were really tight gaps between the games because they had to get it decided – just a couple of days in some cases. Cloughie was their manager, but we finally got the win at the fourth attempt – away as usual. We didn't like taking advantage of being at home! True to form, we'd thrown away two 1-0 leads as well. And we'd already played Forest in the League in January too!

So there we were in mid-February, away to Everton in the Fifth Round, but unlike them we'd already played seven games to get there! We'd still had League games in between too. And those were the days of smaller squads and only having one sub. The words "squad" and "rotation" weren't frequently used back then! It was just game after game after game. And we pretty much always used to travel on the day of the match too. But we had a great time on the coach. It didn't seem to tire us out. I was 21 and was fit as a fiddle so it didn't bother me in the slightest. I distinctly remember standing there at Goodison Park waiting to kick off. One of the Everton players shouted out, "Come on lads, this lot must be knackered, this'll be easy." I thought, "Well, I'm certainly not knackered!"

Generally speaking, we were a pretty young team – apart from Mooro and Mullers, of course. I was 21, John Lacy was a year older, so was Mitch. Les and

Jimmy were about two or three years older. We had a lot of games, but we had the legs for it. Forest and Hull had both been in our division, but Everton were in the First Division – and not just that, they were also top at the time. A big crowd, a top club – it was the kind of occasion you wanted as a footballer. We'd played so many games and made it so hard for ourselves and yet we kept coming back from the dead. But I don't think we ever felt we'd lose, so getting drawn against Everton didn't faze us at all.

We played really well in that match, went 1-0 up through Viv Busby – a two-yard special. They got the equaliser, but that didn't worry us because we were playing so well. The winner came from a move I started down the left. I played it to Jimmy Conway who cut it back at a really tight angle for Buzza to stick it away. He was on fire – he'd already got two in the last Forest game. So you could say that if there'd been no Buzza, there'd have been no Wembley.

The term wasn't around at the time, but today it would have been reported as a giantkilling. It was big news and a big deal for us to beat the form team from the League above. But as much as anything it was just a relief to have beaten a team in one go! It was after that game that we started to get an inkling that it might just be our year. I mean, we were only one game away from the semis at that point.

The draw for the quarter-final was made straight after the Fifth Round. It was live on the radio. We were all sitting there in the bath after beating Everton, and for the first time we were actually conscious of who else was left in. And then it came out of the hat. Away to Carlisle. There were a few swear words muttered, I can tell you – we'd already done about a thousand miles by then! Apparently Alec Stock didn't know we had a radio in there and wanted to come in and tell us who we'd got. But he bottled it because he was worried he'd get soaked when we found out how far we had to go! But we were in the Quarters. And we were really starting to think about Wembley.

Carlisle were in the top division too, but luckily there was a three-week break in between the Cup games which was a pleasant change for us. Today people talk about the Cup being a break from the League, but for us it was the opposite! The quarter-final was played in the first week in March. We were absolutely murdered up there – they slaughtered us. Peter Mellor kept us in it almost single-handedly. They had about eighty per cent of the play and about two dozen shots on target! We just couldn't get out of our half. But Peter was unbelievable – he was plucking them out of everywhere! We were all thinking, "Bloody hell, where on earth did he pull that one from?"

And then came the break. There was a mix-up in their box where the keeper and the defender both left it for each other and collided, and Les Barrett was on hand to poke it into an empty net. The thing is, although we were getting hammered, we weren't getting beaten and we just had this sense that something was on our side. That was the attitude throughout the whole run. When it takes you three games to beat Hull, four to beat Forest, when you go to the League leaders and beat them, and then go to Carlisle, get absolutely pasted and still win, you start thinking to yourselves, "hang on a minute, we might be on our way here!"

There was just under a month between the Carlisle game and the first of what would be two Semis. When the draw was made we just didn't want West Ham because it was a London club, but we didn't have any preference over the other two. When Birmingham came out, there was a genuine sense of "Great, we can win this one…" They had a pretty decent team too – Trevor Francis, Gordon Taylor, Kenny Burns, Howard Kendall – but that didn't intimidate us at all. The way things were going for us, we genuinely felt we could beat them.

By then the Cup had completely take over our season. I mean, before a league game it was business as usual, but we were starting to do a lot more press interviews and Alec didn't seemed to mind. But then we also wanted to keep our form, both as a team but also as individuals because if you played badly you might lose your place. The feelgood factor spread through all the games – we were going out with real confidence every week, and although we picked up the odd draw, we hardly lost around that time.

The first semi-final was up at Hillsborough. That was a rare overnight stop for us. Before we got kitted up, Alec Stock told us to go out on to the pitch and savour the atmosphere. That was an incredible moment that's been etched on my memory ever since – 55,000 people there. I remember looking around thinking, "blimey, this is it…" It really felt like we'd reached the big time.

We went a goal up through John Mitchell – and it was a great goal, too. He kind of set himself up for a long-range volley from the edge of the box and then went charging into the crowd in celebration! I'd been told to mark Trevor Francis out of the game. He'd just been injured, but he was in the England team by then so he was always going to be trouble. Alec said to me, "If you don't touch the ball, I don't care. Just keep him away from it. If he goes for a piss, follow him!" So I went up to Trevor before the game and said, "Hello, I'm your shadow…" And Trevor groaned, "Oh no…you're not one of those players are you?"

I had a great game that day – I just followed Francis everywhere. But then there was that mix-up in our box and, even though we were dominating, they got the equaliser and forced the replay. We were absolutely gutted after that. It was easily the best game I ever played in, both personally and in terms of the team performance. We battered them and we should have won, and at that stage we started to wonder if we'd thrown away our big chance. We'd caught a decent Birmingham team on a bad day and couldn't have played any better ourselves. I think Alec was feeling the same way too, not that he let us know. But, and it was a big but, we still hadn't been beaten.

Four days later on the Wednesday we went back up north to Maine Road for the replay. We were still training in between, but only ball work. We didn't need to do much on fitness because we were playing so much. As we expected they were well on top in that game – we were slaughtered. They came right at us from the off and looked much more like a First Division side than before. But Peter Mellor played really well once again and Mooro was magnificent at the back.

But again that magic was with us. By the time we got into injury time and were still tied at 0-0, there was this overwhelming sense that the game wasn't over. We didn't say anything to each other, but we all knew instinctively that we could do it. By that stage in a semi-final, it doesn't matter who's the superior team. It becomes anyone's game. They were all tired, but we just didn't seem to be – we were running on something extra. We might have been under the cosh, but we were still in it, and while we were, there was always that chance of winning. And then John Mitchell's famous goal went in – which was about as clumsy as his great strike in the first semi was skilful!

I couldn't really believe it at the time. I just remember Mooro screaming at everyone to get the ball away from our area, get it down the other end of the pitch, hit the corner flags. I wasn't really in the habit of just hoofing it, but a ball came to me and I just booted it as hard as I could. I didn't really like doing that, but I think I excused it under those circumstances! And then the whistle blew and the reality of what was happening dawned on us all. We'd played 11 games but we'd got there to Wembley, the Mecca of football.

There were loads of press and TV cameras in the dressing room afterwards. And all I could think was, "I should be crying now." But I wasn't emotional at all, almost to the point where I was actually very conscious of how blasé I seemed to be feeling about it. Everyone else was going berserk and I was ridiculously calm for some reason. In hindsight I think I was numb to what was going on. It was a lot to take in and I don't think I could really believe it.

When you look back, the Final couldn't have been scripted any better. Some Finals just have that bit of extra magic and romance about them, and this was one. To start with, it was West Ham, Mooro's old club that he'd only left a year before. So there couldn't have been a more perfect Wembley swansong for him, although you'd never know it! "Mooro, isn't it great we're in the Final?" He'd be like, "Yeah, it's all right…" He was a very stoic character. You could never gauge his emotions. But it couldn't have been better for him.

Then of course there was Mullers, a Fulham boy through and through. Fulham were the team he supported as a kid, Johnny Haynes was his idol, it was where he'd started his career, and for him to captain the club's first Wembley appearance in one of his last seasons as a player was so fitting. All the more so that two nights before the final he was named as Footballer of the Year. Not bad for a player with a Second Division team – and what's more we wouldn't have even been there if it hadn't been for Mooro and Mullers. Although the rest of the players were decent, it was those two who gelled everything together. If you'd have taken them out the side would have fallen apart, especially in those do or die moments. A couple of wise old heads who've been there and done it makes all the difference. Mooro was by far the best player I ever played with and Mullers was a very close second – and he was a fantastic skipper too. I learnt a lot from him that I put into practice when I became Fulham captain. The fact that one person can influence a game, that a captain can drag his players through if they're having a bad time. He was a great striker of the ball too – never missed a penalty in his career.

And then of course there was our manager, Alec Stock, who was an absolute gentleman of football. We all respected him so much – he'd done so much for football as a whole and for Fulham. He'd been a manager for thirty years and never been to Wembley so this was a big, big deal for him too. And there he was pitting his wits against West Ham's John Lyall who'd only been in management for nine months!

The three of them together – Mooro, Mullers and Stocky – were elder statesmen of the game. As much as we were all delighted to be in the Final, I genuinely think we were more pleased for those three than for ourselves, we really were. As I said, the script couldn't have been any better.

By now the whole of Fulham was in the midst of Cup fever. We were doing so many press interviews – and we were getting paid for them which was a real novelty! All the money got paid into this Cup pool which would be split up later on so you knew you'd be making a few extra quid. And we were getting Cup bonuses too as we got through each round and they were mounting up. So for a 21-year-old like me, things couldn't have been any better. We were going to Wembley to play in that one game that every footballer dreams off, and the money was rolling in. In the end I actually bought a house on the strength of the Cup run – not in cash I hasten to add. I didn't turn up with a bin liner full of notes…but it certainly helped with the mortgage!

We only had four League games between the last Semi and the Final itself. By then our League season was pretty much over – we knew we'd finish mid-table. But ever the professional, Stocky wasn't having any slacking in the side. "No pulling out of tackles so you don't get injured," I remember him telling us. "I want you all playing the game properly or I'll drop you…" Ironically, I distinctly remember making a mental note of that. I wasn't going to lose my place after coming this far and I knew that if you went in half-heartedly you'd be more likely to get hurt anyway. That wasn't going to happen to me.

So then the Portsmouth game came, our second to last home match of the season, with the Final at Wembley two weeks away to the day. Halfway through the first half came that tackle with George Graham. As I said before, it wasn't dirty – my studs just got caught in the turf. I heard the knee tear there and then, but had no idea that it was serious. I didn't even get much treatment because it didn't really hurt that much. Once I was up I ran back and turned, totally unaware of what was going on with the ligaments inside my left knee. As I did, I felt it go again. That was when they pulled me straight off. As I hobbled along the track with the physio a few of the fans were shouting "It'll be okay Les, as long as you're fit for the Final…" I had no idea at the time of the magnitude of what I'd done because it really wasn't that painful. When I got into the changing rooms they put a plaster on it and gave me crutches, but even then, the medical people kept telling me it was only precautionary, so I really wasn't particularly concerned.

A few days later I was called up to the manager's office. Even though I was in plaster, Stocky told me he'd give me every chance to get fit and make the Cup Final side. He actually organised a day out at Wembley for us the week before the big day, just to get us in the mood. I'd had the plaster off by then, and while all the lads were up in the famous Royal Box practicing their victory salute I was jogging round the Wembley pitch trying to get fit!

A few days before the game I was told to go out on to the Cottage pitch and kick a ball around. I was just over by the corner flags with Alan Slough and Jimmy Conway. I went to pass the ball using my right foot, just an easy ball. But my left knee gave way and that's when I knew that it just wasn't going to be. I looked up and to this day I'll never forget Alan Slough's face – he looked absolutely gutted for me.

I was mortified. It was a few days before the biggest game in the club's history. We'd done so much to get there. I'm even choking up now just thinking about it. As I limped into the dressing room Mooro was sitting there. He knew what was happening and he just said, "Strongy, I'm really sorry." I got changed and then Stocky called me up to his office. "Sorry about that," he said, totally matter of fact.

"Nothing you can do about it, but we'll give you half of the Final bonus." I was like, "great…thanks, boss…" It was a nice gesture all the same, but money really wasn't the issue! The bonus was the last thing on my mind. In hindsight I think that Stocky and the medical team were being quite shrewd. What they basically wanted was for me to be able to tell them I wasn't fit rather than the other way around. I remember Mullers saying to me at the time, "You could make out your leg's okay. But if you do that you'll not only let yourself down but you'll be letting the team down." And he was quite right.

By this time, the rest of the lads had finished training and had all gone home so no-one else really knew – as far as they were concerned I still had a chance. When I got home I rang John Fraser. John was a good mate of mine – we'd come up through the youth team together. He'd been in the side as a full-back in place of John Cutbush who'd been injured. So until I was ruled out, there was always going to be a big decision for Stocky to make. Was he going to bring Cutbush back, which would have been our strongest team, or should he leave Fraser in, who'd been doing quite well? But my injury solved that problem there and then. So I called Fraser up and told him he'd be playing. He told me how sorry he was and I'm pretty sure he meant it – mind you he was probably sitting there at the other end of the phone thinking "YES!!!!"

Although I wasn't a part of the actual preparations for the game, I was still around the place all the time and Stocky tried to keep me involved as much as possible, doing interviews and things like that. Stocky never spoke about West Ham that much – as far as he was concerned, it was more about us than them. I remember Mullers constantly telling everyone that Wembley was no place for losers. And he'd know having been there enough times. But we'd done so well in reaching the Final that I couldn't help but sense that getting there seemed to be what it was all about for us. As if that was enough, and that it didn't really matter whether we won or lost, which of course it did. It wasn't a cut and dried thing – nobody actually said any words to that effect. But you could sense it and maybe that pre-empted the result. We'd given blood to get that far with our never-say-die attitude. But getting to Wembley seemed to be the holy grail, rather than actually winning the Cup. It was almost as if everyone felt that we'd done enough already.

Maybe when you're the underdog the best option is to get out there, enjoy it and not worry about the opposition – sometimes that's the only way you stand a chance of doing well against a superior side. But the build up to the Final was very different to any of the other games, even the Semis. A couple of days before the game, Stocky announced, "Lads, we're going out today on a bus around the streets of Fulham to give you the feeling of what it's like to be in a Cup Final." It was incredible – every single road had banners and bunting going from windows on one side of the street to windows on the other – literally every single street in Fulham was like that. And people were coming out of their houses and cheering us and singing. The place was literally gripped with Cup fever. But maybe that was part of the problem. Perhaps other teams would have gone round and done that after, win, lose or draw. Whereas we were almost celebrating just being there.

We stayed in the England team hotel in North London the night before the match. I remember Stocky sitting everyone down and saying, "If I see one player waving to his wife in the crowd, I'll pull him off!" I roomed with Mullers that night – we'd been room partners all season. As soon as we closed the door and put our bags down, he turned to me and said, "I just want to tell you, I'm very sorry you're not playing. I've been to Wembley many times and the chances are you won't ever get there again, and if I could change places with you, I would." He really meant it too. And, unfortunately, he was absolutely spot on!

Because I wasn't playing, I had to leave the lads after breakfast on the morning of the game and go over to the Old Bailey of all places to represent the club in a court hearing. At the start of the season we'd all signed this contract with a boot manufacturer called Stylo which said that, if we were to do well, we'd all end up with a couple of quid. I don't think anyone had asked me to sign anything before that so we all just signed away without reading it! Then, as soon as we got to the Final, Stylo got the contract out and reminded us that we had to wear their boots. Thing is, none of us wanted to wear new boots on the day so we told them we weren't doing it. They then came back with a pair of Adidas that they'd stripped of the markings and stuck their own on, and suggested we do it this way. But Mullers and a few of the senior players were still saying no.

Eventually they took us to court and the hearing was on the morning of the game! There was even talk that the Cup Final was not even going to be played! So there I was, sat there in the Old Bailey waiting to see if there was even going to be a Cup Final! In the end Adidas sued Stylo for defacing their boots. But the verdict from the Judge that morning was that there would be no markings on any of our boots or bags in the Cup Final. If you watch the video of the game you'll see that all the Fulham boots have got their markings blacked out with dubbin. Even Ron Woolnough, our physio, had to have the Adidas logo blacked out on his medical bag and ended up losing out on a couple of grand as a result!

I got back to the hotel in time to get on the coach to Wembley. We had a camera crew on board, and a very young Martin Tyler. Spirits were high and there was lots of banter. I was trying to stay involved, but I couldn't help but feel a bit out of it. As we turned up Wembley Way there were Fulham fans covered in black and white everywhere. It was just incredible. Johnny Haynes was in the dressing room before the game, just to give a bit of moral support I suppose, but the banter was still flying and it everyone seemed very light hearted. Only one or two were showing signs of nerves. John Cutbush was definitely one of them, but he got like that before every game.

The lads took a lot of confidence from Mooro and Mullers. They'd been there so many times before – something like five Wembley Cup Finals between them, and all victories. Mooro didn't seem to offer any insights into West Ham, but we didn't really have any particular tactics specific to the game – it was very much a case of business as usual. We had a formation and a certain style of play that we'd used all the way through – getting it out to the wingers and getting down the line – and that was what we were sticking to. It was a 4-2-4 really – Les Barrett and Jimmy Conway on the wings, Viv Busby and Mitch up front, Mullers and Sloughie in midfield. Cutbush was right-back, Fraser left-back, with John Lacy and Mooro in the middle and Peter Mellor in goal. The whole idea was that, if the ball was on the left, Conway would drop back and if we were on the right, Barrett would drop. So even though it was 4-2-4 on paper, it was more like a 4-3-3 when we were playing. Mind you, Les and Jimmy were the two worst defenders you could have when they did drop back. We weren't really a kicking team anyway. I mean, Mooro and John Lacy would dig a few. But the likes of Les and Jimmy couldn't kick their way out of a paper bag!

With about an hour to go, Stocky said, "Right, just the players now." I was gutted. I totally understood that it had to be like that, but I felt very detached. So I walked out on to the pitch. The tunnel end was where all the Fulham fans were, and as I emerged they gave me the most amazing reception. I was feeling so down at that point, but that made me feel a whole lot better. It was actually very touching.

Watching the game, I was in a bit of a daze. I was sitting about two rows back from Stocky and Bill Taylor, the coach. I was next to Ernie Howe who hadn't made the team either. The game just seemed to be going by in front of me, and I wasn't really enjoying it to be honest.

We got off to a great start which lasted pretty much through the whole of the first half. It was all us – we were completely bossing the midfield and that was no mean feat considering they had the likes of Lampard, Bonds and Brooking. Ironically enough, it was a little known young defender by the name of Kevin Lock who was keeping us out at the back. Not that we knew it at the time, but a few seasons later would come to Fulham and end up making over 200 appearances for us.

There was certainly no lack of confidence amongst our lads – there didn't appear to be any signs of nerves and everyone seemed to want the ball. But I think that's because we'd done all the hard work and were just there to enjoy ourselves. In retrospect, that was our peak if you like. We did as well as we were ever going to in the first half, and if we'd have scored and made the most of the pressure and dominance, it would have been a different game. But again, I just felt that we didn't have that killer instinct we'd seen in previous rounds.

I didn't go into the dressing room at half-time. I left them to it. If I'm honest, I knew we'd had our chances by that stage and that, if West Ham scored in the second half, they'd go on to win the game.

And then the goals came. Two in four minutes, and both originated from that right-hand side. Our right-back, John Cutbush, had been having a good season and there was no doubting he was a good player. But if the occasion had got to anyone, it was him.

Peter Mellor would probably hold his hands up and say that he should have done better for both the goals, and that he maybe should have held on to them instead of parrying them. And perhaps in purely professional terms he's right. But even though he still takes the lion's share of the responsibility for the result I really don't think it can be blamed entirely on him. Overall, he didn't have a bad game by any stretch. Watch it now and you'll see he made a few good saves too. And he had a great Cup run – we wouldn't have even been at Wembley if it wasn't for him. For someone who kept something like 20 clean sheets all season, it's a real pity he seems to carry the can, because it really was more of an inconsistent game for him than a poor one.

I like Pete a lot – he's now a coach for US Soccer, working with the American national team. But any time I've been in his company over the last 20-odd years, someone always seems to bring up the Cup Final and imply that it was down to him in someway. "What about that goal that went through your legs?" And Peter laughs about it. But, you know what? I think he feels it, even now. It still hurts him. Okay, he might have done better, but I really don't think anyone blames him for losing the game. We lost because we just weren't as ruthless as we had been in the other rounds.

When that first goal went in, it really put the game in West Ham's hands. I don't think our heads dropped, but we had a mountain to climb – if you watch the game now, the commentator says exactly that. And from the bench, I just couldn't see a team with the players that West Ham had throwing away a lead. Their fans were going mad and getting right behind them too. All you could hear was *I'm Forever Blowing Bubbles* in the second half. I don't think it was a coincidence that the second went in so soon after. The writing was on the wall by that stage. When you go behind it's amazing how the fatigue sets in. Wembley tires players anyway. The build up saps you emotionally, but the pitch at that time had a reputation for draining the legs. And then psychologically, to have had all that dominance, but to then find ourselves two goals behind all of a sudden…it's pretty hard to raise your game. After that the rest of the game just got played out.

Of course it was Alan Taylor who was our nemesis that day. And having scored two in the Quarters and two in the Semis, he kept the trend going on the big stage with that brace in the Final. It really was his fifteen minutes of fame. He'd been with a relegated Rochdale the season before and had only played a handful of games for West Ham before appearing in the Final. But he just seemed to be on this purple patch. And then about a year later he disappeared as quickly as he'd arrived! Ironically enough, if I'd have been playing I'd have marked him. I know it's hypothetical, but I'm convinced to this day that if I had, he would never have scored two. Three maybe, but not two!

Then the final whistle blew and it was all over. After the lads had been up those famous steps to get their medals from Tommy Trinder, Mullers made a point of rounding everybody up with that famous saying of his that had become so commonplace in the build-up. "Come on lads, let's get off the pitch. This is no place for losers…"

The dressing room was pretty flat. As I walked in, John Fraser looked at his medal, closed the box and held it out to me and said, "Here's your medal…" I couldn't take it off him. But it just goes to show how much they were still looking out for me. Back in those days each team only got 12 medals. Not even the manager got one. But good old Tommy Trinder contacted the FA and explained my situation and how I'd played every game en route to the Final, and in the end they granted me an extra medal. I'm not sure that's ever been done since.

After the game, Stocky was very philosophical about it. He just said, "Oh well, it's been a lovely old journey." That just summed it up really. It was getting there that had been the achievement for us. I think that famous picture of Mooro and Mullers coming off the pitch with their arms around each other tells that story perfectly. Of course they were gutted to have lost. Mullers in particular hated losing. But there were no tears. Like all of us, it was being there that mattered.

As we were getting on the coach to head for the post-match bash at the Dorchester, there were still a few Fulham fans milling about. "Oi Strong!" came the drunken shout from one of them. I'll never forget what he said. "You bottled it! You should have been playing!" I was like: "Great, thanks…"

As the evening went on, the lads seemed to get over the worst of it pretty quickly. In the end a load of the West Ham players turned up at our do – they were having their own one up the road, but apparently it was really dull so they came to ours instead. James Mason, the famous actor, came down too. He was mates with Mooro and was sitting on our table. So there I was as a 21-year-old sitting at the same table as James Mason and Bobby Moore – I couldn't believe it!

We won a lot of friends that season, and even though we lost the Final, we certainly didn't disgrace ourselves. But there are two things that stand out in my mind to this day that say it all. Not once during the Final did the ref reach into his pocket to pull out a card, and not once did either of the trainers have to come on to the pitch to treat an injury. Even though it was a more compelling game than people sometimes give it credit for, that just shows that it wasn't a do-or-die game for us.

I haven't really watched the Final that many times since. It's just doesn't feel like part of my actual Cup run, even though it's the game I've become most known for. There were even two versions of the programme printed – one had me in the Fulham squad and was part of a run that was done before Portsmouth when I got the injury. And then they changed it and printed the rest with me taken out and put John Fraser in. But I don't have either. It's the run that matters most to me, not the Final and it's still a record that'll never be beaten. These days, of course, penalties have stopped rounds going to anymore than a replay, but I don't like to see games sorted out that way. I know there are logistical problems and fixture congestion and I appreciate that you can't have replay after replay like we did back then. But I still like the idea that you let the football decide. I wouldn't have changed any of those games for penalties.

We actually had a replay of the Final in 1995. Fulham were in financial trouble so we made a big deal out of the 20th Anniversary of the Cup Final to raise funds for the club. We managed to get a lot of the old team back together – the only ones who didn't play were Mooro (he had a pretty good reason for not being there after all...) and Mullers, who was too old by then. So he just stood on the sidelines and shouted at us! I managed to play in that one – and we won it, so what does that tell you??!

I watch the FA Cup with interest every year, and it happens every single time with each team that makes it all the way. "So and so will miss the FA Cup Final..." There'll always be some poor bloke who gets injured or suspended at the worst possible time. And every year I think, "You poor sod, I know just how you feel." Yeah, I felt sorry for myself. But I wasn't the first, and I certainly won't be the last.

Oh and by the way, just don't mention the Cup Final!

GORDON DAVIES

STRIKER 1978–1991

BORN   3rd August 1955, Merthyr Tydfil
SIGNED   1 – March 1978 from Merthyr Tydfil; £4,000
              2 – October 1986 from Manchester City; £45,000
FULHAM CAREER (two spells)   450 games, 178 goals
(Fulham's record all-time goalscorer)
HONOURS   Promotion from Division Three 1981-1982, 18 Wales caps
LEFT   1 – Transferred to Chelsea, November 1984; £90,000
        2 – Free transfer to Wrexham, August 1991

The former trainee teacher from Merthyr learned quickly in his first spell at
the Cottage, laying the foundations of a club record 178 goals, 159 of which
were in the League. He was lured to Stamford Bridge by our big-spending
neighbours, but returned to the Cottage two years later after an unhappy spell
with Manchester City. Was with Wrexham when they beat Arsenal in the Cup
upset of 1992, but is still most remembered at his imperious best bagging goals
whilst wearing white.

Birmingham City 3 v Fulham 4

Division Two
Saturday 18 August 1979

St Andrew's
Attendance 19,179

Rookie Welsh forward's opening-day hat-trick proves a false dawn for the club's season

Teams

Neil Freeman	1	Perry Digweed
Jimmy Calderwood	2	Les Strong
Mark Dennis	3	Tommy Mason
Alan Curbishley	4	Terry Bullivant
Pat Van Den Hauwe	5	Richard Money
Malcolm Page	6	Tony Gale
Alan Ainscow	7	Peter Marinello
Tony Evans	8	John Beck
Keith Bertschin	9	Chris Guthrie
Archie Gemmill	10	Kevin Lock
Kevin Dillon	11	Gordon Davies

Evans 28, Dillon 32	**Scorers**	Davies 51, 75, 80
Bertschin 35		Guthrie 60

Referee: M Peck

I'VE ENJOYED SOME truly memorable games with Fulham, and was lucky enough to score one or two goals along the way. To be honest it was a close call between this game and the terrific 4-1 win at Newcastle in October 1982 as to which one to choose; I suppose the clincher was getting the first hat-trick of my professional career. There are plenty of decent strikers who have notched a stack of goals in their careers, but have never managed a hat-trick; it's a special achievement and I was lucky that I managed to break that particular duck quite early in my Fulham career. The other telling factor about that particular afternoon, of course, was that we got the win the hard way – after having been three down at the break.

It was the start of my second full season with the club. I'd arrived in March 1978 from my home-town club of Merthyr Tydfil in the Welsh valleys and had played a part in the final few games of that season. In fact an incident in my first full match, at Blackpool, probably influenced me more than I knew at the time. Just a few minutes into that game I gave away a penalty – and that's why you barely saw me in our area from that day to the end of my career!

Fortunately things worked out for us, and me, at Blackpool. Ray Evans, a superb captain, calmed me down – I was upset as their experienced defender Peter Suddaby had played for the penalty and I guess I was the fall guy – and I managed to set up Les Strong for an equaliser. Les then repaid the compliment by crossing for me to score the winner, my very first goal for Fulham, with a crisp left-foot volley.

George Best had left Fulham earlier that season, and by the time of the Birmingham encounter we had the player the press had touted as "the next George Best" (when he'd come down from Scotland to Arsenal) playing for us. I'm talking about Peter Marinello of course, and he was instrumental in our dramatic victory.

We'd played Birmingham at Craven Cottage in the Anglo-Scottish Cup ten days earlier and had been trounced 5-1. They had just signed Archie Gemmill and, although in the latter stages of his career, he was instrumental in that defeat, buzzing around in midfield and using that special left foot of his to dazzling effect. The Birmingham contingent probably thought they would get another walkover in the league match at St Andrew's, our opening Division Two fixture of the 1979-80 season.

And we were probably only too aware of that possibility as well. Mind you, it was a pretty even first half an hour or so, but then they made the most of Archie's passing ability and the skills of Alan Curbishley and Alan Ainscow to rattle in three goals from Evans, Dillon and Bertschin. As we trooped in for the expected rollicking from Bobby Campbell, it seemed very much "game over". St Andrew's has never been the most welcoming of grounds and their supporters were making a right racket while some of our fans, disappointed at our apparent capitulation, had already set off for home.

Bobby Campbell didn't disappoint. In fact he tore into us. There's no way I can repeat precisely what he said, as this book wouldn't get printed otherwise! Let's just say the dressing room was treated to a full range of expletives, asterisks and exclamation marks! And he was right. A number of home truths were offered, and it was up to us to react. We had to show what we were made of and, at the very least, make a contest of it.

Yes, Birmingham were a good side, and yes they were tough and rugged when they needed to be, and yes we only had three outfield players over six foot in our ranks – Chris Guthrie, Tony Gale and Richard Money. But we needed to get at them a bit more and play to our strengths. No-one was seriously contemplating winning the game at this stage, it was more a case of damage limitation. But after that fearsome blast from Bobby, we were all determined to do much better in the second half.

And that meant giving Peter Marinello more service. There was no point having him on the pitch if he wasn't given the ball. Peter, on the other hand, had to show that he was ready and willing to up his game. He'd been kept pretty quiet in the first half by Mark Dennis. In those days, of course, a defender could put in a hefty challenge or two and get away with a talking-to from the referee. And Dennis was never one to duck out of a tackle. Peter needed to rise to the occasion as a prime supplier to the forwards. The rest of us, too, needed to get our act together. And there was a definite resolve to put in a better team effort, all the time hoping for a break or two.

In fact we put on something of a masterclass in the second period. We knew we were a reasonable footballing side but, with nothing much to lose, we really tore into Birmingham, who themselves must have thought they just had to go through the motions. No doubt their team talk had been of the "you're in the driving seat, keep things tight, don't give anything away especially not an early goal" variety.

In the event, six minutes after the restart we were back in the match. We won a corner and assumed our positions. In training we'd worked out a corner ploy that involved a near-post flick-on, and sure enough, in came the ball from Kevin Lock, Tony Gale flicked it on and I was well placed to get my head to it. I was a few yards out, but was able to get a good connection on the ball; with the pace already on it, the ball flashed over the keeper before he could react. The two defenders on the line could only stand and watch. 3-1. Perhaps it wouldn't be a hammering after all…

The goal gave us the fillip we needed. It was important that we got the next goal – if Birmingham netted a fourth they'd be off and running again, whereas if we got one we'd not only be right back in the game at 3-2, but also the home side's resolve would be tested. With an hour gone Peter Marinello jinked down the wing, beat Jimmy Calderwood and sent in a fine cross. Chris Guthrie still had a lot to do – in fact the ball came a little behind him – but he was such a fine header of the ball that he managed to adjust his body in mid-flight before thumping the ball beyond Freeman with a sort of backward diving header.

Chris was a good leader of the line and wonderful with his head, but we had to work a little at our striking partnership. That wasn't the way with Dean Coney a couple of seasons later – Dixie and I seemed to hit it off right away. Chris was very effective, as his goal at St Andrew's demonstrated, but if anything he'd be so confident with his head that he'd go for goal even from 18-20 yards out when I felt he ought to be looking to set up a colleague. Usually me! That was the only time we'd have words.

The momentum of the game had now changed. We were still a goal behind, but we now had the edge. With 15 minutes to go Peter skated clear again and sent in a cross. I must say that, for his second-half performance, Peter deserved 11 out of 10. He was doing exactly want you wanted from a winger. When you know that the ball's going to be crossed with regularity in a game, then we forwards could take more of a chance – you could make your move anticipating, expecting the ball to come your way. That meant you could attack everything and then it would just be a question of who'd be strong enough.

I made such a move as Peter pinged it over; the ball was travelling towards me and one of their, much bigger, central defenders – Malcolm Page, I think. The keeper was advancing off his line and was three of four yards away trying to take up a decent position. It was simply a case of going for it and hang the consequences. I took a bit of a buffeting – I remember being slightly winded – but the important thing was that the ball ended up in the net, finally getting there off Mark Dennis. But who cared? We were level.

If you look back at that team, we could all play a bit. There was a real desire to play the ball around if we could. The likes of Tony Gale and Richard Money in central defence epitomised that, as did the full-backs, Strongy and Tommy Mason. John Beck was a terrific workhorse and great passer whose influence was very strong in our second-half resurgence, while both Kevin Lock and Terry Bullivant could also pass the ball well. Kevin had a great left foot while Terry, if anything, was one of our more defence-minded players, ready to break things up, although not so meatily as the likes of Roy Keane. If you take a peek at photographer Ken Coton's goal round-up in our following home matchday programme, you'll see that, as that third goal goes in, the nearest player to the action, perhaps hoping for a parry from the goalkeeper, was Strongy. What the hell was our right-back doing up there? That's how positive we were as the game progressed. A little cavalier, if you like, but it worked on the day.

At 3-3, Birmingham were shell-shocked. They'd seemed set fair for their first win of the season, but we were now in charge. And there was a clutch of Fulham supporters by now on a train heading out of Birmingham unaware that we'd drawn level! Of course, the majority who stayed behind were in their element. Having clawed our way back, you might think there'd be the temptation to shut up shop and take the point. But our attacking instincts came to the fore, and rightly so given that the home side were now on the back foot.

There were nine minutes left. I can't remember who played the ball up to me – it was probably John Beck – but I was off in the inside-left channel. Time for a clear head and to rely on a striker's instincts. It also helped that we were playing with real confidence by this time, and I felt I couldn't miss. As the keeper advanced, I went for the far post and drilled it low across Freeman. The ball took a slight deflection as it went past him, but went on to nestle in the net. Time for a little celebration!

The dressing-room afterwards was full of smiles and all very different from 45 minutes earlier. Bobby Campbell, when he was smiling, was like a cuddly teddy bear – it was only when he was in shouting mode that it was best to stay well clear! He was grinning like a Cheshire cat and it was a brilliant feeling. The mood was best summed up, however, when I was given the match ball to mark the hat-trick. Ken Coton was on hand to capture the moment and everyone wanted to be in the picture – that was fair enough, as everybody contributed – and the joy is there for all to see. I may well have scored three goals, but that's what I was there to do. The team spirit was excellent and the supply to the forwards, in the second half at least, was brilliant.

I don't think my mind is playing tricks with me, but the way we knocked it about in that second half was on a par with the very best passing sides, such as Arsenal and Liverpool. Unlike those two, however, we weren't able to maintain it over a season. It certainly helped that we had nothing to lose, mind you. We had a free-flowing style and a positive attitude that hardened into a steely resolve and bolstered confidence levels as the goals went in and the home side visibly wilted.

On a personal level, grabbing a hat-trick was a confidence-booster, too. It doesn't matter at what level you play, scoring a few goals does wonders. I was still very much a novice in the professional ranks so it was a great feeling to score three and to be given the signed match ball. Something like that boosts morale and gives you a big lift for the next run of games. Then again, what the hell do you do with signed match balls? Sue, my wife, wasn't too keen on this one going on the mantelpiece at home sticking out like a sore thumb, so into a plastic bag it went, and then up into the loft. (The ball that is, not the wife!)

The win raised our hopes for the season, but, as it turned out, it was a pretty horrendous one all in all. For all the talent available – Gerry Peyton returned to take over from Perry Digweed and Gary Peters was signed in time for our second match, while Teddy Maybank and Ray Lewington joined later in the season – we were relegated.

By the following October, and with Fulham having made a poor start to life in Division Three, Bobby Campbell was sacked. He was replaced by Malcolm Macdonald, who, aided by Ray Harford, blooded a number of youngsters and put together a bright, attacking Fulham set-up that ultimately almost took the club into the top flight.

Malcolm guided us back into the Second Division. I had a new strike partner in Dean Coney by then. We had an almost telepathic understanding right from the off. Dixie brought so many people into play with his intelligent work as a target man. He never was a 20-goals-a-season striker, unfortunately – mainly because all his goals seemed to be absolute belters. He never seemed to get the scruffy type of goals that probably accounted for 20-30 per cent of my tally – and people are very quick to criticise one or two of his high-profile misses, all the while conveniently overlooking those he did score and the dozens he set up.

From the Birmingham game, only Tony Gale, Kevin Lock and myself were still in the team against Newcastle. It was my 200th game, actually, and it turned out to be a destruction of one of the most fancied sides in the division. They were even helped out by a couple of dubious spot-kick decisions – Kevin Keegan scored one and missed another. In the meantime we knocked the ball around almost for fun and made a few people sit up and take notice of what we could do. It was a tragedy that the side that contained the likes of Gerry Peyton, Paul Parker, Robert Wilson, Roger Brown, Ray Houghton, Geoff Hopkins and Ray Lewington didn't make Division One. It was just as great a tragedy that the squad was broken up so soon afterwards.

I didn't get a hat-trick up at St James's Park! Just the two, with one being judged BBC's Goal of the Season. Ray Houghton also scored a beauty, a wonderful lob, and Dixie grabbed the other.

One of the things that Malcolm introduced was subtle, but vital, as far as I was concerned, and came from his vast experience as a striker. He encouraged players to slide the ball up to an attacking player where he would ideally want it – and that's not necessarily to his feet, but perhaps just to one side. If played correctly – and we had a number of great passers in the side – that would give me a split-second's advantage, not having to control the ball and then turn, but simply turn onto a well-weighted pass.

Those first few seasons at Fulham were crucial for me. I very quickly developed a magnificent rapport with the supporters. I don't know whether it was because I played with a smile on my face, put in plenty of effort or simply because I was knocking in a fair share of goals, but they have always been very, very good to me.

It was difficult not to bond with the club. It has rightly been known as a friendly place and, as I later found out in spells with Chelsea and Manchester City, it's not the case everywhere that you're pals with everyone from the tea ladies to the board members, admin staff to the youth teamers. Certainly I felt a great affinity and was genuinely grateful they offered me the chance to play professionally.

I didn't find out until a little later that the club had been offered an opening bid of £350,000 for me the season after that Birmingham match. We'd played West Brom a couple of times in the Cup and their manager Ron Atkinson came in for me. It seems he wanted me to partner Cyrille Regis and play in the same side as Bryan Robson, Laurie Cunningham and Remi Moses. They were a more than reasonable First Division outfit and it would have been an interesting proposition – but then football's full of such twists, turns and "if onlys". Bobby Campbell turned the offer down, and maintained his stance even though the offered transfer fee went up to £400,000 and ultimately £450,000. Not bad for a someone picked up from South Wales for £4,000 – a figure that in today's market wouldn't buy Alan Shearer's big toenail!

It's a very different footballing world nowadays with very few players sticking with one club for any length of time. You can understand that, I suppose, with bucketloads of money available at the top level of the game. Any move means a lot more money in the coffers and, if I'm honest, if I was playing today I'd be only too happy to at least listen to such offers, given that a footballer's career is relatively short. But during my first five or so years at Craven Cottage the thought of actually leaving the club wasn't an option. I was so very grateful to Fulham for giving me my chance that I felt I owed them some loyalty. The only way I could repay Fulham was to give it my all, learn as much as I could along the way and, as a striker, stick the ball into the back of the net as often as I could. So I did.

ROGER BROWN
CENTRE-HALF 1980-1983

BORN 12th December 1952, Tamworth
SIGNED March 1980 from Norwich City; £100,000
FULHAM CAREER 161 games, 19 goals
HONOURS Promotion from Division Three 1981-82
LEFT Transferred to Bournemouth, December 1983; £35,000

Roger was a bean-pole of a centre-half as committed to the cause as he was
to having a good time. A natural leader, Roger was the defensive rock around
which the 1982 promotion side was built. He also notched a dozen goals,
mostly from set-pieces, and his down to earth attitude – he'd come into the
game late after working in engineering – was invaluable in the dressing room.
After finishing his playing days at Bournemouth, he left the pro game after an
unhappy time as Colchester boss, but is fondly remembered at the Cottage for
his fearless team leadership.

Fulham 1 v Lincoln City 1

Division Three
Saturday 18 May 1982

Craven Cottage
Attendance 20,398

Blood, sweat and tears as last-day win takes Fulham back to Division Two

Teams

Gerry Peyton	1	David Felgate
Jeff Hopkins	2	David Carr
Les Strong	3	Phil Neale
(Sub. Dale Tempest)		
Sean O'Driscoll	4	Glenn Cockerill
Roger Brown	5	Trevor Peake
Tony Gale	6	Steve Thompson
Gordon Davies	7	George Shipley
Robert Wilson	8	Phil Turner
Dean Coney	9	Gordon Hobson
Peter O'Sullivan	10	Tony Cunningham
Ray Lewington	11	Stuart Hibberd

Brown 58	**Scorers**	Carr 72
	Sent Off	Thompson 57

Referee: E Read

THE LINCOLN GAME – am I sick of people asking me about it? No, of course not, even though every time I attend Fulham or football-related events it's always the subject that arises. It is a turning point in the club's history, the first promotion in 11 years and only the fourth since the war, I believe. The way it came about made it all the more exciting, like England versus Australia in the cricket at Edgbaston in the summer of 2005! It's a one-off pressure situation, the kind that probably won't repeat itself in a generation. And I can assure you I never get fed up with talking about it.

It was our 46th and last league match of the 1981-82 season, played in front of our own fans at the Cottage. The crowd was over 20,000 – twice that of the season's previous best. Burnley would be crowned as Third Division champions that year, but the other two places were still up for grabs as the season drew to a climax. Three sides were still in with a shout. As luck would have it two of those faced each other at the Cottage that afternoon.

Lincoln, who had 76 points, needed to win to ensure promotion as they stood a point adrift of us, while we could get away with a draw and still ensure we finished in third. The Imps had stormed up the league with a late flourish, putting together a 16 game unbeaten run from February to mid-April.

Our form was less good. We'd won just two out of the last six games, although one of them had been the previous Wednesday, 3-0 at home against Preston. The other team in the equation were Carlisle (alongside us on 77 points), who had looked nailed on certainties to win the division until three defeats and a draw in their last four games brought them back into the mix. They were away at Chester, a team that had already finished miles adrift at the bottom of the division. So it looked like United would get a result there, leaving us and Lincoln to slug it out for the final promotion place.

The support that year had been fantastic, and I'm not just talking about this game in particular. I used to be inspired by those fans. You couldn't compare the Fulham faithful with Manchester United and Newcastle – I'll admit they were quiet by comparison, who isn't? – but that day it was like running out into a cauldron. They made me feel ten feet tall. As a player, you don't usually get time to think about things like that – you could be on a park pitch, most of the time for all the noise you actually take in from the stands while you are concentrating on the job in hand – but we'd had good support all year. The key that afternoon was that it was all or nothing for both clubs, though I don't recall Lincoln bringing down too many fans.

I'd enjoyed a good relationship with the Cottage crowd ever since I signed for Fulham Football Club just before the 1980 transfer deadline. I was ever-present for two seasons, 1981-82, and 1982-83, and played 39 games in 1980-81, but my first match in March '80 was a devastating experience. I signed on the Thursday, we played local rivals Chelsea on the Saturday and I tore my knee ligaments just before half-time. I realised something had happened and tried to play through the pain, but came off with ten minutes to go. Hence I went into plaster and missed the rest of the season.

I'd left Norwich, then a top-flight outfit, after a bit of a set-to with manager John Bond, who'd brought me there from my first professional club, Bournemouth. When Fulham boss Bobby Campbell came in for me, Kenny Brown, the assistant manager at Norwich, quietly advised me it would be best if I didn't stay. I spoke to two or three clubs, but felt Campbell was the kind of bloke I could play for. He paid quite a lot of money for me as a centre-half – a six-figure sum, I believe.

Fulham had bought me to shore up the defence and try and help avoid relegation from Division Two, but unfortunately we got relegated and I went into the history books for playing consecutive games in three different divisions – Norwich in the top flight, Fulham in the Second (the defeat to Chelsea) and then my next game was in the Third. That made *A Question Of Sport*, can you believe?

I came back for the first game of the 1980-81 season, but things weren't going well and Bobby Campbell was sacked after the September/October period had brought six straight defeats and just one goal. In a surprise move, Malcolm Macdonald left the commercial office to take charge of footballing matters in his place. When there's a change of management it's a worrying time for most players. But I was 25, 26 at that time, I'd been late turning professional, so it wasn't as if I feared losing my job. But then again I was confident I'd retain my place because I was good enough. It didn't bother me!

The only thing that did bother me was the reaction of the other players and Malcolm, being a totally different kettle of fish from Bobby Campbell, took a lot of the pressure off the youngsters. People like Jeff Hopkins, Paul Parker and Tony Gale could start expressing themselves without fear of doing something wrong – Bobby would have hung them from a Cottage coat peg!

Malcolm wasn't capable of bollocking people or even raising has voice. This was his first spell at management. That's not to say he wasn't a good manager, but he would probably admit that when he took over he didn't know how to manage! He was lucky to have the likes of Ray Lewington and myself at the club, old heads who could bring the youngsters along and nurture them. That's why we had success.

George Armstrong, his ex-Arsenal colleague, was Macdonald's coach in the first instance and Ray Harford came along a little bit later. The three of them were there for the promotion season of 1981-82. When we went up we played in the Second Division and the following year we just missed out on playing in the First Division, the equivalent of today's Premier League. That was a good season – but '81-82 is the one I remember most because I scored a lot of goals.

There was a secret to my success, a free-kick routine we worked on in training. It involved me, my central defensive partner Tony Gale and Dean Coney, who was playing up front with Gordon Davies. There were a lot of teams who didn't know how to defend against it – or, even if they did, couldn't handle it. We worked on it over and over again and it worked a treat against Lincoln.

We would take up positions which would eventually leave me with a bit of open space. Tony could put a ball on a sixpence from a set-piece, so it was necessary for someone to hit that space and make it count. Tony took the free-kick, Dean would make the first run and I would make the second run. He would block off my marker – unselfish of him, you could say, but then again Dean wasn't as good in the air as me!

Later on, I coached schoolboys at Eton public school and tried to teach them the tactic, only to be reprimanded by their headmaster who said "We can't cheat!" Blocking the player off is a form of cheating, I suppose…so fair do's.

Les Strong had been captain under Bobby Campbell; when Malcolm came in, Les was captain for part of the year, then he gave it to me. As club captain, I was expected to play a different role to just a team captain. You'd look after the young-sters off the pitch as well, if we were away from home, or if something needed sorting out in training. I'd been about a bit and I think a lot of the players looked up to me; that stood me in good stead if I needed to do anything.

There were many times Ray Lewington and myself would get at the back of the team coach and, if something had gone wrong, sort it out between us. I think it was a kind of gelling that all managers want, and I think Malcolm was lucky to have senior players who could give the others a good hiding if they weren't working hard enough! He would leave us to our own devices and, barring injury, the team would pick itself week after week.

The important thing was that players were quite open to criticism, even myself. It gelled ever so well, and it continued the following year, as when we beat Newcastle 4-1 at St James' Park. Another great day…and a familiar sounding result for modern Fulham fans!

Tony Gale and I were complementary characters in every way. I was the ball-winner, the hard man if you like, and he was the pretty boy who would sweep up around me. He wasn't the bravest of players, but he had a good brain and intelligent feet – what I didn't win he would pick up. When I speak to him now he still says he made me what I am and I always say I made him what he was! We had a good working relationship. Then we had Strongy at left-back – a good, steady player who was never going to set the world alight, but was reliable.

Gordon Davies up front was probably the laziest centre-forward there was, but Ivor was always in the right place at the right time. Young Dean Coney, inevitably nicknamed "Dixie" after the Everton legend, was the workhorse alongside him. Then there was Gerry Peyton in goal, who was big and stable – so right down the middle we had a spine built for success.

We picked up Ray Houghton from West Ham reserves the following season, but it was former Welsh international Peter O'Sullivan who gave us experience at this time. And Ray Lew, in the middle of the park, was a bit like a "mini me". He was a small centre-half playing in midfield who would win the ball for you. Robert Wilson, next to him, developed before my eyes – he played better and better every match. But in the games prior to Lincoln we had been losing points and it was always going to come down to the wire. In our favour was the fact that we had a side that believed in themselves and had experience to match.

Sean O'Driscoll, who completed the four-man midfield, would be running in the 90th minute the same as he did in the first – he had bellows for lungs, I still don't know how he did what he did. He worked hard, he was never a great goalscorer, but when the goals needed to come Sean was there…he got four in eight games during the run-in, though I'd insist on telling him he missed ten times as many as he scored! We lost Gordon for a few games and Dixie as well, and he stepped in to fill the void they left. Robert Wilson scored a few as well.

We used to call Sean "Noisey", as he was such a quiet lad. But the quiet ones often go the furthest. When I left Fulham to go back to Bournemouth I took John Beck, Gerry Peyton and Sean with me, and he's still there as manager today. He became a physio and then, because of Bournemouth's monetary circumstances, they had no choice but to give the job to Noisey – and he's done well.

Jeff Hopkins had come in at the end of the previous term and played most of the season, winning the Number 2 shirt back off Kevin Lock. He hadn't fully developed physically at that time; the following year was more his season. Kevin Lock, who came from West Ham, was a player who could play in defence or midfield. He was injured at Gillingham two matches from the end, allowing Jeff back in and Les Strong to switch flanks to the left (Locky being a left-footed player).

But Kevin's absence on the day almost cost us dear, because Les wasn't really fit enough to start. He'd missed out on the 1975 Cup Final, as he himself tells you elsewhere in the book, so you can understand why he wasn't keen to do it again. I pulled him into the Cottage treatment room before kick-off and said "If you let me down because you're not fit…" He told me he wouldn't but, as it turned out, he didn't even last the first half. And, at that time we were down to the bare bones with injuries.

Malcolm called me over to the touchline and I said "Les can't carry on." The Lincoln right-winger had been running rings round him, cos he'd been limping for a while, and I remember thinking we'd have to make three or four positional changes to accommodate Dale Tempest, the reserve centre-forward and the one man on the bench that the rules then permitted. Malcolm decided to go for a straight swap and put Dale at left-back and he did ever so well; we were lucky that worked out.

The sending off of their centre-half Steve Thompson for his second booking 12 minutes after the break – he'd picked up his first clattering Gerry early on – gave us the chance to work our famous free-kick routine. Tony put it in the mix, Dixie blocked the marker and my header went in off the bar. But in all honesty I think them going down to ten men worked against us. We had our backs to the wall in the second half, we were bombarded. It got pretty physical and I ended up with both my eyes and my mouth split open.

It was probably right that defenders should claim both goals, as both side's forwards were locked up good and tight, and when they scored the equaliser after 72 minutes we were rocking. Their right-back Dave Carr scrambled it in after a corner. Everybody was coming forward. They had nothing to lose as they had to beat us to be sure of promotion and were throwing everything at us. You have to remember the age of our side at that time. We had a lot of kids and some of the youngsters' arses started to twitch and they sat back a bit. I remember the last 20 minutes we lost a little bit of our shape and were defending all the time. The pressure was enormous both mentally and physically.

The centre-forward playing against me, Tony Cunningham, was a right big physical git. I gave as good as I got as sometimes when you play hard against somebody they'll hide a bit, go away. He didn't – he kept coming back for more. I'd played against him before, it had always been a contest. I knew I was going to get a smack in the mouth with the elbows, which was common practice in those days. He was one of the most physical players I've ever faced, but that was my bread and butter – I enjoyed it.

I remember Thompson and Cunningham best; they'd been around a while and Thompson was a centre-half like me. It was a bit ironic, as a few years later I applied for the Lincoln manager's job before I went to Colchester.

There were other coincidences surrounding that game and those players too. Two youngsters lining up against us would return to the Cottage as comparative veterans – Glenn Cockerill, then a young wing-half, who played in 1996/97 for Fulham under Micky Adams, and keeper David Felgate. In 1998 he came back with non-League Leigh RMI and played a blinder to win them an FA Cup replay.

When the final whistle went I was too exhausted physically and mentally to do anything but collapse. There were a few tears, too. The pressures leading up to the game had been immense. I remember trying to make my way off the pitch afterwards with the crowd running on and patting me on the back. I gave my shirt, covered in blood, to one little lad. He's still got it, he's 29 now, I spoke to his mum a year ago. I got in the dressing room and had that cup of tea you see me drinking in that famous photo by Ken Coton – but I'll let you into a secret, it wasn't tea in that cup. It was whisky!

I didn't get up to the Cottage balcony with the rest of the lads as I had to get stitched up real quick following my battle with Cunningham – 12 in each eye and six in the cheek, inside my mouth. That's what the whisky was for! They had to stop the bleeding. So I missed out on the celebrations. Come to think of it, I think I just made the sixth curtain call…

Just to complete the picture, Lincoln were pipped to promotion by Carlisle, who scraped a 1-0 win at Sealand Road and finished second. It just shows how vital it was that we held out. And we managed it.

Fast forward 12 months and we were playing another one-off game for promotion. But the match at the Baseball Ground was something else – a massive, massive occasion, but in all other respects the total reverse of Lincoln. It was marred by the fact that some of our players got beaten up by so-called Derby fans as they left the field. There was a threatening atmosphere. We were never going to win that day. We didn't deserve to, we didn't play well enough, though we only needed another goal which could have happened at any time. The fact there were still four to five minutes to go when the referee blew the final whistle only added to the misery.

That game and that promotion was actually lost six weeks earlier on transfer deadline day. We'd been about 14 points clear of everybody, miles out in front, and the critical decision that Ernie Clay, the chairman at the time, made was when Brian McDermott came on loan from Arsenal. They wanted £100,000 to sign him permanently and Ernie wouldn't pay it. Malcolm had brought him in when we needed that little bit of a lift and Brian gave us exactly that. But we needed to keep him till the end of the season and we let him go back. After that we struggled and struggled: we started losing games and drawing games. Three defeats in a row towards the end allowed Leicester to catch us and then it came down to Derby.

The team was the same as the previous season with a couple of exceptions: Locky had replaced Les Strong and Ray Houghton, O'Sullivan. It's like anything else, what could have been and what might have happened. We all knew we had everything in place, but with Brian not signing, some of the heads went down and we lost all the advantage we had. We wasted it, really…if we'd won another game or got another four points over the season we'd have been promoted no matter what had happened on that dark day at the Baseball Ground.

The year after, I think Ernie Clay knew he was going to leave the club and he wanted money. He sold everyone he could: I was the first to go and the whole team followed me. A lot of people ask me why I left – I didn't leave voluntarily. I never wanted to leave Fulham. I loved the club, loved the supporters and my heart is still there – I'd still be there today if I could have been. Ernie had obviously asked who was disposable and Malcolm was determined he didn't want me; he thought I'd served my purpose and that was his choice. I didn't want to stay somewhere I wasn't wanted, and when Harry Redknapp of Bournemouth came in for me as player-coach I thought I had no option but to go. I wanted to play, and it was with a heavy heart that I left Fulham.

Ironically when I came back to Craven Cottage nearly three years later it was to be offered the now vacant manager's job. I was offered the job only to be let down at the eleventh hour and this is another story that those in the know have offered me money to tell. It was an embarrassing time for me. I was just leaving Bournemouth as a player and went through all the negotiations with the then chairman David Bulstrode; Ray Lewington would be the player-coach and I would be the manager. The press conference to announce us was set for 12 o'clock on the Saturday. I met Ray in Richmond Park that morning: we talked tactics and what we would do pre-season, so on and so forth. I spoke to Bulstrode on the phone about 11.15 and said I'd see him at a quarter to 12.

We went up to the Cottage and the press was there in force. All of a sudden Bulstrode called Ray in: he came out, looked at me with heavy eyes and then I was called in. Bulstrode said "I've decided we can't afford to pay both of you: Ray can play, so I've made him player-manager." That took me years to get over, in fact I still haven't. I'd have been a good manager here, but that's life for you. And to this day I haven't a clue why Bulstrode changed his mind. I have my suspicions. Let's say if I ever bumped into the current Southampton manager again I would probably be doing community service!

Manager Dugald Livingstone (right) meets (from left) me,
Jimmy Hill, Tom Wilson and Johnny Haynes, on the banks of the
Thames to plot the downfall of Cup holders Newcastle

Poor old Ian Black; if only he'd tipped the ball over the bar
then centre-forward Vic Keeble (right) would never have had the chance
to bundle him into the net for their winning goal

FULHAM FOOTBALL CLUB

SEASON 1955-6

PRO CIVIBUS ET CIVITATE

OFFICIAL PROGRAMME

4d

F.A. CHALLENGE CUP, 4th ROUND

NEWCASTLE UNITED

SATURDAY, JANUARY 28th, 1956

KICK OFF 2.45 P.M.

I reckon this was just about the best game of football
ever seen at Craven Cottage. It must have been as people
are still talking about it half a century later!

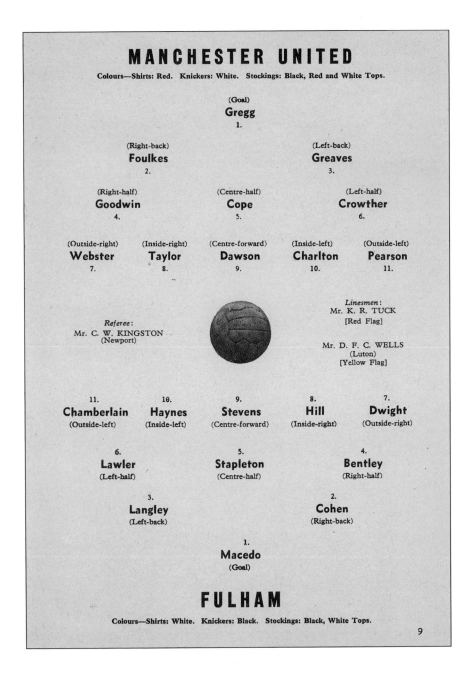

MANCHESTER UNITED

Colours—Shirts: Red. Knickers: White. Stockings: Black, Red and White Tops.

(Goal)
Gregg
1.

(Right-back)　　　　　　　　　　　　(Left-back)
Foulkes　　　　　　　　　　　　　**Greaves**
2.　　　　　　　　　　　　　　　　　3.

(Right-half)　　　　(Centre-half)　　　　(Left-half)
Goodwin　　　　　**Cope**　　　　　**Crowther**
4.　　　　　　　　　　5.　　　　　　　　6.

(Outside-right)　(Inside-right)　(Centre-forward)　(Inside-left)　(Outside-left)
Webster　　**Taylor**　　**Dawson**　　**Charlton**　　**Pearson**
7.　　　　　8.　　　　　9.　　　　　10.　　　　　11.

Linesmen:
Mr. K. R. TUCK
[Red Flag]

Referee:
Mr. C. W. KINGSTON
(Newport)

Mr. D. F. C. WELLS
(Luton)
[Yellow Flag]

11.　　　　　10.　　　　　9.　　　　　8.　　　　　7.
Chamberlain　　**Haynes**　　**Stevens**　　**Hill**　　**Dwight**
(Outside-left)　(Inside-left)　(Centre-forward)　(Inside-right)　(Outside-right)

6.　　　　　　　5.　　　　　　　4.
Lawler　　　**Stapleton**　　**Bentley**
(Left-half)　　(Centre-half)　　(Right-half)

3.　　　　　　　　　　　2.
Langley　　　　　　**Cohen**
(Left-back)　　　　　　(Right-back)

1.
Macedo
(Goal)

FULHAM

Colours—Shirts: White. Knickers: Black. Stockings: Black, White Tops.

9

Of United's semi-final line-up only Harry Gregg, Bill Foulkes
and Bobby Charlton had survived Munich, so it really was a
wave of emotion that got their new team to Wembley

Tony Macedo might not have covered himself in glory in the semi-final replay, but without him we wouldn't have been there in the first place. Here he saves a flying header from Charlton's Johnny Summers in our fourth round win at the Valley

(From left) Johnny Haynes, Jimmy Hill and Roy Bentley board the train to Birmingham in eager anticipation of the FA Cup semi-final

Jimmy Hill beats Ray Wood to put us ahead at 2-1 in the first game.
We were in dreamland!

It was a gloomy Wednesday afternoon at Highbury, but that didn't stop
the Fulham public queuing in their thousands. Sadly it wasn't to be and
Wembley would have to wait for a visit from Fulham for another 17 years

We were always chasing the game, although when Arthur Stevens netted our first I still thought we were in with a decent chance

Poor old Tony Macedo; he'd been outstanding in our cup run, but had a nightmare at Highbury. The young Bobby Charlton hammered the final nail into our coffin to make it 5-3, beating Tony at his near post with a low shot into the far corner

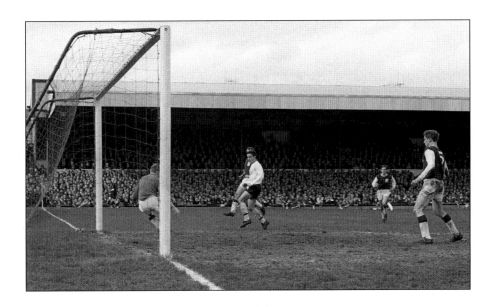

We'd gone in 2-1 down at half-time and as they say, cometh the hour, cometh the man. It was definitely my hour and the chances came my way

My second goal was a towering header – or so I keep telling everyone!
It was good enough to find the net anyway

What a way to round off my hat-trick.
Having soaked up Northampton's pressure we broke clear and I just
had to take it round the keeper and slot home

I'm sure if Kenneth Wolstenholme had been commentating he'd have
used his "There's some people on the pitch" line to describe the joyous
scenes of celebration amongst the Fulham fans at the end

JOHN MITCHELL — 1975
BIRMINGHAM 1 FULHAM 1
& BIRMINGHAM 0 FULHAM 1

FULHAM

versus

BIRMINGHAM

CITY

1-0 John Mitchell celebrates Fulham's goal

F.A. Cup Semi-Final Replay

at Maine Road, Manchester Wednesday, April 9, 1975 kick-off 7.30pm

Official Programme 15p

1-1 Joe Gallagher celebrates the equaliser

I love this programe cover from the replay. It's got a great shot of me celebrating my goal from the Hillsborough game

In that first match I cracked in a half-volley to put us 1-0 ahead...

...and raced to celebrate with the fans

The 120th minute of the replay. It felt like time had frozen.
The ball dribbled so slowly over the line.
But I didn't care that it had come off my midriff.
I'd just taken Fulham to Wembley

Fulham Chairman Tommy Trinder knew a thing or two about

We were all well up for any old stunt after the elation
of winning that semi-final. Even taking the mickey out of our
opponents in the final, West Ham, by posing in the tub
at Craven Cottage blowing a bubble or two

I had plenty of time to kick my heels before
the Cup Final and so got roped into all sorts of things
including signing the "Good Luck" rosette…

…and defending the club in court over the strange case of the boots with no advertising! In the end the lads' Adidas sponsored boots got blacked out for the match and all because of that company called Stylo

It was a strange feeling, being in the dressing room at Wembley with all the boys, but knowing I wouldn't be involved. Skipper Alan Mullery told me that he would have gladly swapped places with me as he'd played at the old stadium many times. I really appreciated him saying that

FULHAM

(Colours: White shirts, Black shorts, White stockings)

1. P. MELLOR
2. J. FRASER
3. L. STRONG
4. A. MULLERY (Captain)
5. J. LACY
6. R. MOORE
7. J. CONWAY
8. J. MITCHELL
9. V. BUSBY
10. A. SLOUGH
11. L. BARRETT

Substitute: J. DOWIE

Manager: MR. A. STOCK

FULHAM'S ROAD TO WEMBLEY

Third Round	Hull City (Home) (Conway)	1–1
Third Round (*Replay*)	Hull City (Away) (Busby 2)	2–2
Third Round (*Second Replay*)	Hull City (Leicester) (Slough)	1–0
Fourth Round	Nottingham Forest (Home)	0–0
Fourth Round (*Replay*)	Nottingham Forest (Away) (Dowie)	1–1
Fourth Round (*Second Replay*)	Nottingham Forest (Home) (Slough)	1–1
Fourth Round (*Third Replay*)	Nottingham Forest (Away) (Busby 2)	2–1
Fifth Round	Everton (Away) (Busby 2)	2–1
Sixth Round	Carlisle United (Away) (Barrett)	1–0
Semi-final	Birmingham City (Hillsborough, Sheffield) (Mitchell)	1–1
Semi-final (*Replay*)	Birmingham City (Maine Road, Manchester) (Mitchell)	1–0

Goalscorers: **Busby 6, Mitchell 2, Slough 2, Barrett 1, Conway (Jimmy) 1, Dowie 1.**

Total 13

It didn't help my feelings that the Cup Final programme was originally printed with my name on the team sheet. In later print runs, they replaced me with John Cutbush, who played in my place

To see the lads walk out onto the Wembley turf and line up to meet the
Duke of Edinburgh without me didn't help the way I was feeling

After we'd lost I tried my best to console everyone in the dressing room,
but I think we all knew that the team hadn't really turned up on the day.
Here Johnny Haynes takes time out to console me on my misfortune

My first professional hat-trick began with this header from a corner

And that's me, bottom to camera, having nicked my second in at the
near post past keeper Neil Freeman and Malcolm Page

I have to thank Ken Coton here for making me look so fantastic in this shot as I ram my third and the winning fourth goal home. Cheers, Ken!

Bobby Campbell hands me my hat-trick ball. It was a shame that doing so well on the opening day proved to be a prelude to a disastrous season

My goal was just one of those headers that I caught perfectly and sweetly
in the middle of my forehead and it flew into the net

Manager Malcolm MacDonald made me his captain that season
and the next when we nearly made it to the First Division

Winning promotion is something that has to be savoured
and I found just the right way – a cigar and a dram of whisky.
I bet you all thought it was tea in that mug!

Wolves had a decent side and would eventually win promotion
back to the top flight that season, but they reckoned without
the tactical nous of Ray Harford, our coach

While winning the game after being 2-1 behind at half-time was great, what was important for me was the footballing lesson I learnt. It really opened my eyes as to how a coach can influence the course of a match…

…and after a recent stint at Watford, I'm now back at Fulham again hoping to do just that

COCA-COLA CUP, ROUND ONE, FIRST LEG

LUTON TOWN V FULHAM

THE HATTERS

LUTON TOWN FOOTBALL CLUB

LUTON TOWN

TUESDAY AUGUST 16, 1994, 7.45 PM

Sponsors of Luton Town F.C.

The Coca-Cola Cup

Official matchday programme £1

Luton may have been two divisions above us, but we had some real experience in our line up and didn't fear them at all

Go on then. Sing that song, the one my daughters now
chirp up with every time they see me in shorts. I like the line about
"worth a million pounds" myself!

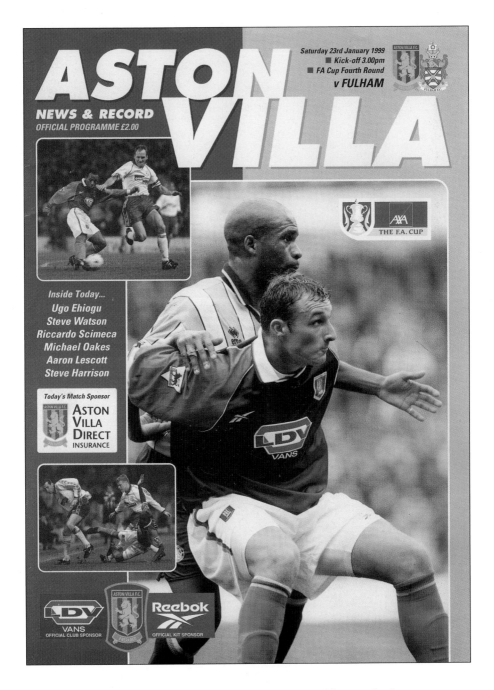

Villa were top of the Premier League and boasted a host
of household names in their side, but we had a game plan and
more passion about us that day

Kevin Keegan was always telling us to play with our hearts, although his hand gestures could be slightly ambiguous. I don't think Villa manager John Gregory was too amused

After my header found the top corner, the next thing I knew I had Pesch clambering all over me. We both had good reason to celebrate Villa losing!

Then Steve Hayward cracked home this free-kick through a
terribly constructed wall and we were home and dry

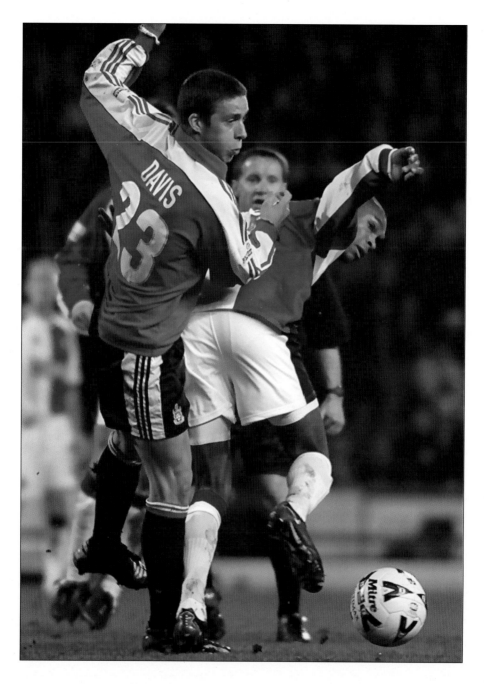

It was a tough game and we had to get stuck in. Unfortunately tempers were on edge and Rufus Brevett got sent off, but we just used that as yet another motivating factor to add to Souness' pre-match bluster

You can see what it meant to both us and the Fulham fans in the background to steal a march on Souness and Blackburn. Nice feeling!

I don't think I'll ever live down the dance I did after scoring the late equaliser against Sheffield Wednesday to win us the title

Chairman Mo loved every minute of that promotion campaign and here he celebrates with the First Division Trophy on the top of our bus during the victory parade

Our game plan was to harass United as much as we could and that meant getting in amongst them early, so I kept the pressure on in midfield by keeping on top of Nicky Butt

Steed makes it 2-0, cracking home Louis Saha's knockdown

Junichi Inamoto beats Quinton Fortune to the ball to clinch
our memorable victory 3-1

Winning at Old Trafford doesn't happen very often so we savoured
every last minute of it

I tried management for size myself at Colchester, but didn't enjoy it – that's when I decided that football wasn't the life for me any more. I was disappointed in what happens behind the scenes, I can't say any more than that. I'd been an engineer, but couldn't go back. I worked with lathes and turning machines; that all went computerised during the time I was in football and left me behind.

When I made my decision to quit after Colchester got an 8-1 mauling from Orient I knew we didn't have a side or a club that could stay in the League. I knew this was the time to get out. I told the chairman what people were trying to do and said it wasn't something I wanted to be involved in. I have never done anything illegal in my life, and there were things going on the average punter wouldn't know about. I took the brunt of it and it affected my family, so I got out.

Happily, my love of football has survived. I do a lot of kids' coaching and took a side in Norwich, where I lived until recently, from Under-9 to Under-16 level. I also do a bit of scouting. I've just moved back to Tamworth where I hail from, where ex-Fulham player Mark Cooper runs the local Conference club, and have had a few coaching offers since I arrived, so who knows what will happen? My football journey started at Walsall, where I was once an apprentice professional, so it's all more or less come full circle for me.

For the past 11 years I've been working for the probation service. It's the same as being in football – I'm helping people to get back on their feet, giving them a second chance. Maybe it's the captain in me. I had a good grounding outside the game, which helped when I had to learn to live without it. When I finished with football it wasn't such a big thing to be on half the money – I started with nothing and went back to nothing. It was no big deal.

I came into football at 24 and came out at 36, 37. I invested my earnings in property, but unfortunately lost all my money in the housing slump of 1989. I put my house on sale when I left Colchester in '89 and sold it in '94. I wouldn't have minded if I'd pissed it up the wall or gambled it away! That's when I decided to go back to college and re-educate myself, and I find myself here 11 years on.

My last memory of that May day in 1982 was going into the Riverside bar and staying there for God knows how long. I knew what promotion meant to the club after so many disappointing years, and especially to the fans. I used to go in the Riverside after matches and meet them. It was a family club, you could get involved with supporters.

Then we went into the city to continue the celebrations and a friend of mine, who's sadly no longer with us, eventually drove me home to Camberley at about five in the morning! I didn't sleep for a couple of days. It was the best day of my life and will live with me forever. Even though I've been lucky enough to have a lot of highlights, only one thing in life has ever surpassed that feeling and that's the birth of my kids – it's the only thing I can equate to it.

RAY LEWINGTON
MIDFIELD 1980–1990

BORN   7th September 1956, Lambeth
SIGNED   March 1980 from Vancouver Whitecaps; £50,000
FULHAM CAREER (two spells) 234 games, 21 goals
as player from 1980-1985, and as Player-Manager from 1986-1990
HONOURS   Promotion from Division Three 1981-82
LEFT   Transferred to Sheffield United, July 1985; £40,000

A no-nonsense midfielder, Ray was brought up a Chelsea player, but has a fascination for Fulham nurtured during his first spell in the early eighties. He returned as player-manager in July 1986 after a year at Sheffield United, and in 2005 Ray made his third appearance at the Cottage as reserve-team coach after stops at Crystal Palace, Brentford and Watford.

Wolverhampton Wanderers 2 v Fulham 4

Division Two
Saturday 20 November 1982

Molineux
Attendance 14,448

*Inspirational half-time team-talk turns the tables on
promotion-hunting Wolves*

Teams

John Burridge	1	Gerry Peyton
John Humphrey	2	Jeff Hopkins
Geoff Palmer	3	Kevin Lock
Kenny Hibbitt	4	Sean O'Driscoll
Joe Gallagher	5	Roger Brown
Robert Coy	6	Tony Gale
Peter Daniel	7	Gordon Davies
Wayne Clarke	8	Robert Wilson
Andy Gray	9	Dean Coney
Mel Eves	10	Ray Houghton
(Sub. Mel Cartwright)		
Mick Matthews	11	Ray Lewington

Clarke 10, Gray 41	**Scorers**	Lewington 26, Davies 59, 73
		Wilson 85

Referee: K Cooper

As I EXPECT most of you know, I started my career as an apprentice with Chelsea. I'm sorry about that. I went on to make the best part of a hundred first team appearances for them, and I thought things were going pretty well. Perhaps I would be with Chelsea for the rest of my playing days. However, when he had been in the job for a few months, new Blues manager Danny Blanchflower decided that he wanted to bring in some fresh faces. He needed to save on money paid to the existing players, so he had a clear out and put six of us on the transfer list.

In 1979 football was becoming increasingly popular across the Atlantic, so I decided to try my luck in Canada by signing for Vancouver Whitecaps. This may have come as a surprise to some, as I was one of the very few young players to go to Canada or the USA. Normally it was the option for players coming to the end of their career. I went initially for a year, with a three-year option, which meant if I didn't like it I could always come back. In fact, I loved it out there and, although I came back to play for Wimbledon on loan, I fully intended to return to Vancouver. We had some good players in our side, we'd won the Soccer Bowl and it was a great place to live.

As things turned out, I couldn't agree a new contract and ended up signing for Fulham on transfer deadline day in March 1980. I knew the Fulham manager, Bobby Campbell. He had bid for me previously, and was apparently upset when he found out I was off to Canada. While I was with the Whitecaps, we came over here for pre-season training at Bisham Abbey. One day, Bobby turned up and said that he'd heard I was having trouble over my new contract. He said he was willing to sign me then and there. That was that: Vancouver sold me to Fulham for £50,000.

The game I've chosen for *Match of My Life* is a Second Division encounter between Wolverhampton Wanderers and Fulham, in November 1982. First though, a few words about the situation at that time, and some thoughts on the Fulham squad during those hectic years. I'll have to be a bit careful what I say about Browny, but it should be okay as we have a pact. I'll be nice about him, if he'll say nice things about me!

When we travelled up to Wolverhampton for that game, we were riding high – as indeed were Wolves. I'm not quite sure now, but I believe we may have been about third in the table, while Wolves were fourth with the same number of points.

They had been relegated from the First Division [then English football's top flight] at the end of the previous season, and were to return to it at the end of 1982-83, only to come back down again a year later. All that was in the future, however, and for now we had to get a result at Molineux to ensure we kept our promotion hopes alive and kicking.

We had, of course, just come up from Division Three in 1981-82, and had a very good squad of players. Malcolm Macdonald was the manager, although he did not get very involved with the coaching, which early on was mainly undertaken by Roger Thompson and, by the time of the Wolves game, was very much in the hands of Ray Harford. Malcolm sometimes came over as a bit fierce, but he was probably the most amiable manager I've ever worked with, and liked a relaxed atmosphere. He got very close to the players. In some ways he was a bit "Brian Cloughish" as he always did things differently to all the others. I remember how one Friday night he insisted on buying all the players a beer. (I can't quite see Arsène Wenger doing that!). One or two declined – but he said they'd got to have one, and that was that.

Our keeper was Gerry Peyton – the most dedicated footballer I've ever played with. He was a great student of the game, and talked about it all the time. When he wasn't playing or talking about football, he would be training. Les Strong was always telling him to put the ball away and go home, but Gerry would just carry on regardless.

Kevin Lock was very laid-back. He had started his career as a central defender at West Ham, but converted to the left-back position when he moved to Fulham. Kevin replaced Les Strong just three games into the season. Taking over from a legend like Strongy was never going to be easy, but Kevin slotted into the side nicely. He was a great penalty taker and he had as good a left foot as you'll ever see. Cool and calm, he never got excited or lost his temper. During his time at Fulham, he missed a lot of games with hamstring trouble.

Roger Brown, meanwhile, didn't miss a game in the 1982-83 season. He was a real captain [He had replaced Les Strong as skipper part-way through 1981/82], and had as much influence off the pitch as on it. He'd stand no nonsense in training – even from the senior players. After the Lincoln game the previous season, he'd become Mr Fulham due to his blood-soaked heroics. The fans recognised his bravery and the fact that he would do whatever was necessary to clear a ball, and they also recognised his never-say-die character on the pitch, although they probably didn't fully appreciate the extent of his professionalism or influence. I won't mention the fact that, after every game, the first thing he would do would be to light a fag! Sorry, Browny. That one slipped out!

Tony Gale was a wonderful footballer. He was a midfield player really, who played centre-back. He was one of few defenders I knew who would step up to take a free kick and curl it in from 25 yards. He had combined with Roger in the centre of the defence to help ensure that we won promotion the previous season. Perhaps only his lack of pace prevented Tony from playing for England.

Sean O'Driscoll had come from non-league Alvechurch three years earlier. He gave us balance on the right-hand side, and when he wasn't playing you realised just how much you missed him. "Noisey", who is an excellent coach, is of course still in the game, as manager of Bournemouth. Another largely unsung hero was Robert Wilson. He wasn't always easy on the eye, but he was quietly efficient and scored some vital goals for us, including a total of 11 in the 1982-83 League season.

Dean Coney was another player perhaps not always fully appreciated by the Fulham faithful. He was very unselfish, and the lads loved him. He scored freely at the beginning, but for some reason couldn't carry it on. He was a brilliant hold-up player, but maybe he was a little bit too nice for his own good. And then there was Gordon Davies. You very rarely play with natural goalscorers like our Ivor. He was one of the very best I played with, only Steve Finnieston of Chelsea coming close. Ivor had the wonderful knack of being in the right place at the right time, and could score goals with just about any part of his body. He was an instinctive player, and his goals got us out of trouble on many occasions. He scored 24 of them in the 1981-82 promotion campaign, and a further 19 in 1982-83.

There was one other vital player in the team of 1982-83: Ray Houghton. Unbelievably, Ray had come to Fulham on a free transfer from West Ham prior to the start of the season. Things are different now, with the way contracts are set up, but in those days you very seldom got a good player on a free, and you certainly never got a player like Ray. His has got to be the greatest free-transfer ever. West Ham made a big mistake when they decided to let him go – you only have to look at his subsequent achievements to realise that.

As a team, we couldn't believe our luck. We went to Ireland pre-season, and the things he was doing were marvellous. We half expected it to wear off after a time – but he just got better! He was a wonderful player, with all the skills and great energy. He played wide left, which he didn't particularly like, but at the time we had Noisey on the right, and Robert and myself in the middle. Ray could both score and make goals, and he was a great team player. Together with Clive Walker, he now does commentaries on English games for Arabic TV stations.

Later on, we were to have Paul Parker, the best of the kids to come through during that period. He had great pace. He was very shy initially, but he had an excellent temperament. He went on to play for QPR, Manchester United and

England, and this came as no surprise to anyone. On the other hand, when Cliff Carr came along some of us weren't sure that he'd make the grade. However, he did very well as a left-back and surprised us all, especially as he was so short for a player in that position. John Marshall joined Fulham as a junior, and was to play his first senior game in September 1983. John is as honest as the day is long, has always had the club at heart, and is Fulham through and through. He was happy to play in any position, and I never heard him complain about anything. John was at the Cottage as chief scout until very recently.

A couple of other players from this period deserve a mention. Peter Scott was always willing to learn, and I think he should have got further with his career. Unfortunately, he was either up in the air when things were going well, or very depressed when they went badly. Leroy Rosenior was always up in the air – usually to head the ball. He looked very raw when he first broke into team, but he really wanted to do well and worked very hard at it. He was keen on extra training sessions – always a good sign. I bought him back when I became manager, but was forced to sell him at a profit a few months later. At least this won't happen to his son, Liam, who is of course now at the Cottage. I suppose I ought to say something more about Les Strong, too, but he was such a quiet, unassuming character with absolutely no personality that I've forgotten all about him…

Now for that game at Molineux. There are two people who have really influenced me in football – Dario Gradi, who was reserve-team manager while I was at Chelsea, and Ray Harford. Ray thought deeply about the game, and, as I say, he was responsible for Fulham's coaching at that time. We had made an excellent start to the campaign and the fans were already beginning to think about the possibility of a second consecutive promotion. A week earlier we had beaten Grimsby 4-0 at Blundell Park, and we'd also won 4-1 at both Newcastle and Middlesbrough earlier in the season. Of course, this was Fulham, so a week before the Grimsby game we managed to lose 3-0 at home to Oldham! I'd like to report that I wasn't playing in that game, but in fact I didn't miss a game all season, so I take my share of the blame for that one.

We arrived at Wolves' ground knowing it was going to be tough for us, and in the first half at least, it definitely was. The footballing expression "under the cosh" most certainly applied. They had some good players in their side, including Joe Gallagher, Wayne Clarke (brother of Fulham's 60s striker Allan) and Andy Gray. Gray, now of course a Sky Sports pundit, was absolutely ripping us apart, and almost every time a Wolves winger crossed the ball, Andy, or another forward, came close to scoring. And in fact that was how Wolves scored both their goals in that first half; quick ball out to the wings and a cross which the strikers could attack in the air. It was inevitable that they'd convert one or other of the chances. As it happens, we were probably fortunate that they only scored twice. In-between times we were playing quite well, but we were losing out in the air – even Browny was having one of those days when little went right.

We were 2-1 down at half-time after I'd brought us back into the game by rounding off a tidy move to net one past the much-travelled John Burridge. But the most important thing about that match didn't even happen on the pitch. It happened at half-time in our dressing room and it completely changed the face of the game.

In those days there really wasn't very much in the way of tactics going on. Nearly every team played 4-4-2 and it was all pretty straightforward. But this was one game where a coach actually changed the course of the game at half-time, hence the reason for my picking this particular match. If things had gone well in the first 45 minutes, most managers and coaches would say something like "Well done. Keep it up". If you were losing, they would simply have a quick rant and call you names – the words "you're crap" come to mind! It was as simple as that at most clubs.

But Ray did something different that day. He recognised that the full-backs had to prevent the wingers getting crosses in, so he told them to stand outside the winger to force him inside. That way, they wouldn't be able to get crosses in so effectively. These days, you do it all the time, but in 1982 that was rocket science! It worked, with Kevin Lock especially taking Ray's words to heart. Wolves hardly put a cross in during the second half. I was amazed. The coach had changed the game at half-time, and we ran out 4-2 winners. For the record, Gordon Davies (2) and Robert Wilson were our second half scorers as we bossed the game. It was amazing. Once we'd snuffed out their threat, Wolves had no other way of hurting us. They were a one-dimensional team. They got frustrated and we got on top of them. We'd been scoring a few goals in the games preceding that one. In fact, as well as the four we stuck past Newcastle and Grimsby, we'd put three past Blackburn and Burnley in the past six games, so we knew where the net was.

What impressed me most that day, however, was that Ray Harford had turned the game around in just a few short minutes. I'd never known that to happen before, and it really started me thinking about coaching, and my long-term future in the game.

We were all naturally elated after that match, and the following week we again played well to beat fellow promotion contenders Sheffield Wednesday 1-0 at the Cottage. Of course, we then went to Leicester City – and lost 2-0! Having helped the team draw 0-0 at Stamford Bridge just after Christmas, I scored against Wolves again on New Year's Day. This time however, we were far from elated – as we lost 3-1. Good old Fulham!

We had these occasional setbacks but, as the campaign wore on, we looked more and more like a side heading for promotion. After we lost that return game against Wolves, we won our next four League matches – at home to Shrewsbury and Middlesbrough, and away to Rotherham and Bolton to sit comfortably in third place, where we stayed for a couple of months. It wasn't until the last few weeks of the campaign that it all started to go wrong. Near the season's end, we lost three on the trot, including a vital game at Queen's Park Rangers, who were to be promoted as champions. So, although we won our last home game against Carlisle with a brace from Robert Wilson, promotion rested on the last day of the season at Derby County. It was a crucial match, with Derby needing a result to be sure of staying up, while we needed to win to gain promotion.

The game turned out to be a disaster. From the start, there was an intimidating atmosphere inside Derby's old, cramped, ramshackle Baseball Ground, but we didn't play particularly well and I think we panicked a bit due to our inexperience. We conceded a goal to striker Bobby Davison and time was running out. Our game had a lot of injury-time and so all the other results were in and we knew we'd need a miracle to go up as we had to win the game to clamber above Leicester and back into third spot.

After a lot of aggravation and threatening behaviour from a large number of Derby supporters, a pitch invasion followed the referee blowing his whistle for a free-kick Their fans believed that was the final whistle and that they had survived the threat of relegation. That caused the game to be abandoned with a couple of minutes left to play. It was a dreadful business, and Jeff Hopkins was seriously assaulted by some Derby fans. It took him a long time to recover from that. The game should have been replayed, and I believe that, if it had been, we'd have won it – and therefore won promotion to the top flight. In the end, we partly had ourselves to blame for a faltering end to what had been a magnificent season, but it was all very sad.

That was the closest the club had come to returning to the top division since those disastrous seasons in the late 60s when Fulham plummeted from First to Third Division on the back of two bottom places in consecutive seasons. We'd played some great football and come so close to promotion, but it wasn't to be.

Things went downhill after that. Malcolm Macdonald left Fulham during the following season, and Ray Harford became manager. Ray's appointment was eminently sensible, but he was on a hiding to nothing. It soon became clear that chairman and owner Ernie Clay was not prepared to put any more money into the club, and decline was inevitable. Mr Clay was, of course, the man all Fulham supporters loved to hate, but in the early days the players quite liked him. We didn't know about the politics going on behind the scenes, and to us he was just a friendly chap who took a real interest in what was going on. In all my years at Chelsea, I'd only ever met the chairman once, and I'd certainly never seen any chairman come down to the training ground to watch the players in action. But Ernie came down to training every day during my first week at Fulham, always carrying his umbrella. If you had a shot which went wide, he'd say something like "I'm paying these lads two hundred and fifty quid a week, and they can't shoot straight." We thought he was quite a character at that time. We also thought £250 a week was good money!

With my playing career beginning to draw to a close, I started thinking seriously about coaching and managing. Ray Harford had really started me thinking about it after that game at Wolves. He always encouraged me, and pushed me to go for my coaching badge, which I got when I was 25. Ray was a great coach and a top man. I was ringing him up until the day he died, asking for his opinions. He didn't generally say a lot, especially in interviews, and what people often didn't realise was that, in private, he was a very funny man.

Ray Wilkins (sorry about all these Rays) once said to me "Everyone's got this impression that he's a dour man, but he's really great fun." Once Ray Harford got to know and trust you, he was fine. He got stitched up by a journalist once, and after that he put the barriers up and became suspicious of everyone. But he helped me out a lot. It was a tragedy for the world of football, and for everyone who knew Ray, when he died at such an early age in August 2003.

Towards the end of my first stint at Fulham, everything went dreadfully wrong. We even lost our training ground and were forced to train without permission next to the Cottage in Bishop's Park. And this was a team playing in the Second Division. I remember on one occasion, when we were due to play Leeds United on the following day, a park keeper turned up, so we picked up the cones we'd been using (I dare say they had been nicked from some local roadworks!) and legged it back to the Cottage. It's hard to believe now, but it's true.

I eventually moved from Fulham to Sheffield United, but never really settled there. Meanwhile, Ray Harford had got the job at Luton and he phoned me to say that the new chairman had asked him to recommend a player-manager for Fulham. He had recommended me, but he then told me, as a mate, that I shouldn't take it because it would be a really difficult one. I thought about it and decided I'd go for it, for once not taking Ray's advice. Ray said he'd put the word about and find an easier one for me – but I said "I know Fulham, and I want to go back there".

I don't think anyone will ever have a harder first job. Not only had the training ground gone, but we had no boots. We couldn't buy anything from anyone, because we owed everyone money – even the local shops. Ray Wilkins had moved to AC Milan by then and he phoned me to congratulate me on getting the job. I don't think he was having a laugh! When I told him about the boots, he sorted out some sponsorship so we could kit out the team. To find a training ground, I got in my car and drove around looking at any football pitch I could find. I found one eventually, and we went to Banstead down near Epsom.

I didn't know it at the time, but the new chairman, David Bulstrode, had no intention of putting any money into the club. Within a few months the merger with QPR was proposed, and then the club almost went out of existence. I had a knee injury, and we were scratching around to put a side together. Amazingly we managed to stay in Division Three, as it was then, although the last day escapology in 1989/90 was cutting it a bit fine, but the club was in dire straits. Eventually, Jimmy Hill came to the rescue, but my days at the club were numbered – for a few years at least.

I went to Crystal Palace as reserve team coach. After a few months I began coaching the first team – they were promoted to the Premier League the year I joined then they went down again. I later became joint manager with Peter Nicholas in 1995/96, with Steve Coppell as director of football. It was something of an up and down existence for Palace at the time, with frequent changes of division and frequent changes amongst the personnel. Then I damaged a knee, which became infected, and I was out of action for a good while. By the time I came out of hospital, the club had been relegated again, and it had also been sold. This was a typical Lewington scenario!

Terry Venables had been made manager. I was offered a role, but former chairman Ron Noades had decided to buy Brentford, who had just been relegated to the bottom division. Ron came to see me in hospital and told me he wanted me to go with him to Griffin Park. Micky Adams was the manager there, but Ron was going to sack him. He didn't say who would actually be managing the club, but he said he had someone in mind. It turned out that he had himself in mind!

So the chairman became the manager, and guess what? Brentford finished the next season on top of Division Three! Although Ron didn't do much on the coaching side – in fact he didn't do anything on the coaching side – he did the buying and selling and he did pick the team each week. I did everything else, but I think he felt he'd made a point, and we certainly had a lot of laughs along the way. In many ways, that was my happiest year in football. Ron eventually got out, and I became manager. After Brentford, it was Watford. At first I was in charge of the reserves, but I also worked with the first-team squad.

Gianluca Vialli became manager, and money was put into the club in an all-out effort to secure promotion. Sadly, the effort failed, Luca was sacked and I was appointed manager of a club which had no money – again! I had three years in the job and finances were really tight. We had to cut the wage bill, rely on free transfers and make all sorts of other economies, but at least we could still afford to buy a few pairs of boots! I think we did pretty well in all the circumstances, and we did get to a couple of semi-finals. I was disappointed to get the sack from Watford, but now I feel I'm back where I belong.

I'm immensely grateful to Chris Coleman, one of best defenders I ever worked with, for bringing me back to Fulham. The changes are incredible. We have a magnificent training ground, and the cones in Bishop's Park are now a distant memory. When I left Fulham, the club was on its knees, but I've come back to a thriving organisation. There seems to be people everywhere, but I've found it easy to integrate, even though there's hardly anyone here that I knew before. The new Fulham is still in its infancy, and there is much still to be achieved with, no doubt, a few upsets along the way. But it's nice to be back home again, hopefully working with many of Fulham's first-team players of the future.

JIM STANNARD
GOALKEEPER 1980–1995

BORN   6th October 1962, Mile End
SIGNED   1 – June 1980 from Ford United
          2 – August 1987 from Southend United; £50,000
FULHAM CAREER (two spells)   430 games, 115 Clean Sheets
(27% of all games)
LEFT   1 – Transferred to Southend United, March 1985; £12,000
        2 – Free transfer to Gillingham, August 1995

One of Fulham's many character keepers, "Big Jim" Stannard re-signed after
a two and a half year stay in Southend for a higher fee – evidence of his value
to the side. After an in and out introduction to the team in the early 1980s,
when Eire international Gerry Peyton stood in his way, Jim became a fixture
in the Fulham team and now holds the club's record appearances for a keeper,
Jim remains a cult figure thanks to his bravery in the early 1990s when his fine
performances often saved a deteriorating team from even bigger hidings.

Luton Town 1 v Fulham 1

Coca-Cola League Cup First Round First Leg
Wednesday 16 August 1994

Kenilworth Road
Attendance 3,287

One-man Stannard show halts Hatters' League Cup progress

Teams

Jürgen Sommer	1	Jim Stannard
Julian James	2	Simon Morgan
Marvin Johnson	3	Robbie Herrera
Ceri Hughes	4	Michael Mison
(Sub. Dwight Marshall)		
David Greene	5	Kevin Moore
Trevor Peake	6	Glen Thomas
Paul Telfer	7	John Marshall
Scott Oakes	8	Duncan Jupp
Kerry Dixon	9	Alan Cork
David Preece	10	Gary Brazil
Scott Houghton	11	Rob Haworth
(Sub. Des Linton)		

Oakes 79	**Scorers**	Moore 88

Referee: R Bigger

First Off, I'd like to clear up one thing. All the books seem to give my birthplace as Harold Hill. I'm not sure why this is. I did live there when I was younger, but in fact I'm a true Cockney lad, born in Mile End, within the sound of Bow Bells.

They tell me I was a Fulham hero during the late '80s and early '90s. During my two spells at Craven Cottage, I notched up what I believe is a record number of first team appearances – 391 in the League, 14 in the FA Cup and a further 25 in the League Cup. I looked this up – fortunately, there have been some good books written about Fulham! My League appearances were all in the lower divisions, but, during my second spell at the club, I'm told many Fulham supporters felt that I could have played at a much higher level. Maybe I wish I'd had the opportunity, but I loved my time at Craven Cottage. We had a blast.

I've always been a big lad, but I think I was pretty agile for my size. I like to think I was brave, as well. When the crowd sang: "He's big, he's round, he's worth a million pounds." I was really chuffed. My two little girls, Amy (7) and Grace (4) have now adopted this song, and will sing it to anyone who is prepared to listen. In fact, they sing it all the time, whether anyone is listening or not.

Quite a few people have told me that Fulham's plight would have been very much worse had "Big Jim" not been between the sticks, during many of the difficult years. Some, I know, were surprised and quite upset when I was given a free transfer by manager Ian Branfoot and subsequently signed for Gillingham in June 1995. In my first season there, I was ever-present, and conceded just 20 goals in the entire campaign – a new Football League record for a 46 game season – and only six goals at home. I also kept 29 clean sheets, another League record. I was voted Player of the Year, and also selected for the PFA Divisional Team of the Year. The free transfer now looks like a bit of a misjudgement, and was seen by many supporters as typical of the way Fulham Football Club was being run at the time.

I always had an ambition to be a League goalkeeper, but I first signed for local side Ford United. Fulham came in for me in June 1980, when I was just 17, but I'd not been at the Cottage all that long when I managed to break a leg. To have a bad injury when you're just getting started in your career is very frustrating, I can tell you. It wasn't much consolation to have my picture taken for the programme, while I was sitting on the dear old Cottage balcony with my leg in plaster. Still, I soon bounced back (no bouncing jokes, please).

I played for the juniors at first. Then, during the 1980-81 season, Fulham went through a particularly rough patch. By January 1981 the team had won only one of their previous 13 Division Three games, and weren't far off the bottom of the table. Manager Malcolm Macdonald had played me in a friendly against Brighton, and now he gave me my League debut at home to Swindon. We won 2-0, with Gordon Davies and Tony Mahoney scoring second-half goals. What a player Ivor was! While I was to go on to break the appearances record for a Fulham goalkeeper, he was to go on to create a new goalscoring record for the club.

However, for now, I had kept my first clean sheet. It was nice to have an average of nought! I kept my place for the rest of the season and, although I say it myself, I did pretty well for an 18 year-old. I conceded one in my second game, at home to Brentford, and then kept another clean sheet at Blackpool. In 17 consecutive games at the back end of that season, I let in 21 goals. I've got my calculator out, and I reckon that's an average of just under one and a quarter goals per game. Fulham finished in a respectable thirteenth position. Quite a revival.

Fulham's regular Number One, Gerry Peyton, was back in the side the following season. He was an excellent keeper who played for the Republic of Ireland (although, typically for them, he didn't seem very Irish to me!) so of course he was going to be hard to displace on a permanent basis. He helped me a lot in my early days, but naturally he didn't help me to displace him. I got only two first team games in 1981-82, and this was the season in which Fulham finished third in the table, and won promotion.

In the early days, I had brief loan spells at both Charlton and Southend. These gave me a bit of extra experience, although I only played in half a dozen League games for Southend, and one for Charlton. Unfortunately, I didn't get to make any first-team appearances for Fulham in 1982-83, and only a handful in the next two seasons. So, in March 1985, Fulham decided to sell me to Southend. I was very disappointed, as I was going from a mid-table Second Division club to one struggling in Division Four. But in those pre-Bosman days us players had no say in transfers, so I was sold and that was that. I went on to make more than a hundred appearances for the Shrimpers, never missing a game while I was there, and proved that I could do a good job.

When I moved to Roots Hall I was told that I'd have to move down the leagues to come back up again, and this was more or less how it turned out. I naturally didn't know that I'd one day be returning to Fulham, but when Ray Lewington decided it was time to buy me back two years later (for more than four times what Fulham had originally got for me) I took the opportunity with both hands. Mind you, it's just as well I did take it with both hands: If I'd only used one hand, I might have dropped it. (I thought I'd get that one in before someone else does.)

Gerry Peyton had moved on to Bournemouth, and during my first two seasons back at Fulham I only missed one league game. The club was in the Third Division, the League consisted of Divisions One, Two, Three and Four at that time, and at the end of 1988-89 we finished fourth to make the play-offs for a place in Division Two. We had two play-off games against Bristol Rovers. We lost by just a goal to nil at their place, and felt we had a real chance to beat them over the two legs. However, things became a bit desperate in the next game, none of us played well, and we went down 4-0. Promotion was therefore not to be, and basically, things went from not too bad to very much worse.

I missed only a handful of games in the next two heart-wrenching seasons, and I like to think that at least I helped to prevent us from being relegated during that awful time for the club. I was again ever-present in 1991/92, when we finished in a much more respectable ninth position, and I kept 18 clean sheets in all competitions. Two seasons later I again featured in every League match, but this time we were to be relegated to the bottom division, our fate being sealed when we lost 2-1 at Swansea. I had just one more season at Craven Cottage before leaving again.

The trouble with being a keeper is that you can play really well in a game for 89 minutes, only for one single lapse to make everyone forget the good bits. Unsung heroes, that's what we goalkeepers are. Still, when you've played more than 700 games for several clubs, it should be easy enough to find one in which you played really well all the way through! In all modesty, I can think of a few over the years, although not all of them were for Fulham. I might have chosen the Fulham game at Crewe in September 1989, when I scored from a clearance, even though I'm told some people believe Andy Sayer got a touch on it on the way in – but in any case I conceded two on that day, so I'll forget that one. The game I've actually chosen is a First Round First Leg Coca-Cola Cup tie at Luton Town, played on 16th August 1994.

Why? You may well ask! I know all footballers say it, but most of us really do treat each game as it comes. Sometimes, it's the only way to stay sane! With the Premier League by then a reality, in 1994-95 Fulham were in the bottom of the four divisions. We did not have a bad campaign in the new Division Three, although we were to have a very poor run in the September before we started to put some League results together, finishing up in a respectable eighth place with 62 points.

The first Coca-Cola Cup game was, of course, played early on, so the League campaign was barely underway (we had played just one game – a 1-1 draw with

Walsall) and we were all still hoping for promotion back to Division Two at the end of it.

Meanwhile, the Coca-Cola Cup was important to the players, and to the club itself. It's perhaps not the most glamorous of competitions in its early stages, but for a club like Fulham at that time, it could produce much-needed revenue. In the second round, you might get drawn against a team from a higher division, and there was always the possibility of facing one of the big name teams in later rounds. In this case, while we were in the bottom division, Luton were riding high in Division One – two whole divisions above us.

We had some very good players during my years at Fulham. The really outstanding ones, like Paul Parker, Tony Gale, Ray Houghton and Gordon Davies, were no longer with us by 1994. They had all gone to pastures new, in most cases to bigger and more successful clubs, but we still had the three Ms – Morgan, Marshall and Moore – as well as others who were capable of doing really well. Even so, few neutrals would have given much for our chances in this match. With a lot of good defenders in the side, you could be forgiven for thinking that our team looks like it had a very defensive formation, but in fact I recall it being a straightforward 4-4-2, with the versatile John Marshall occupying a midfield role.

Johnny was a true professional if ever there was one, and could play as a full-back, a central defender, a midfielder and even, on occasion, a striker. Duncan Jupp was a 19-year-old full back, who won Scottish Under-21 caps and went on to join Wimbledon, while Glen Thomas was a very good central defender. Kevin Moore was another central defender and a great organiser, who had a good career behind him, firstly at Grimsby and then in the top flight with Southampton, and was almost twice the age of young Duncan! Robbie Herrera was an attacking full-back, who signed for Fulham from QPR. Rumour had it that a mystery Fulham fan had stumped up the transfer fee for Robbie. Those were the days!

The midfield contained Gary Brazil, who was to become Fulham's youth team coach a couple of years later, Michael Mison, a tall lad who perhaps never quite fulfilled his early promise, and Simon Morgan. Of course, everyone knows there's only one Simon Morgan! Up front, we had Wimbledon veteran Alan Cork, who was still capable of knocking in the goals, and Robert Haworth, who didn't return to League football after leaving Fulham a while later and then, sadly, breaking his leg.

Considering our league status, we played some excellent football that night, as did Luton, which, in the circumstances, was only to be expected. The thing I liked about Kenilworth Road was that they always watered the pitch before a game.

Provided it's not overdone, this is always good news for goalkeepers as it makes landing a lot less painful – especially for the heavier ones among our brethren.

Mind you, there can be too much water on the pitch – I once almost sank without trace at Northampton's Sixfields Stadium, when I stepped onto what appeared to be a solid piece of ground during the pre-match warm-up, only to find the lower part of my left leg disappearing before my eyes as the turf gave way. A lot of people thought it was funny, and to be honest so did I, but it could have been very dangerous. Footballers get quite enough injuries without having to contend with the ground disappearing beneath their feet. Apparently, the fact that the pitch had been used for rugby was to blame as they'd simply covered the holes that the posts made with flimsy board and laid turf on top. Classy!

I think I'd better return to the Luton game, or you'll get confused. The first half was full of incident and both keepers had important saves to make. All in all, we were putting in a very good performance. As a footballer and, I think, particularly as a goalkeeper, you sometimes get the feeling that this is your day and that you are going to give an outstanding performance. That was how I felt that evening when I stepped out at Luton. I made a one-handed save from Kerry Dixon early on, and then saved a fierce shot from David Preece midway through the first period. In between times, Corky fired just wide for us, following an excellent cross from the right by Robert Haworth.

With a 0-0 scoreline at half-time, we all felt that we had a real chance to win the tie overall, and perhaps even to win that away leg. Both teams created a number of goalscoring opportunities during the second period, but I just seemed to make save after save. There were top-corner saves, one-handed saves and one-on-ones. I remember one in particular, near the bottom of the post. I'm not quite sure now whose shot it was, but I think it must have been the first one from Kerry Dixon. I do know that I was completely amazed that I'd saved it. In fact, I wasn't at all sure that I had, but somehow I got my hand to the ball before it went over the line and turned it round the post.

In the second period both myself and Luton keeper Jürgen Sommer, who was an American international, had to make some spectacular saves. At the other end, Gary Brazil almost scored, while I saved one belter from Scott Oakes. Then, unfortunately for Fulham and for me, Oakes at last beat me with a 25-yard screamer, about ten minutes from the end. To be honest, I was devastated, as it seemed that all the good work had been for nothing. However, I'd reckoned without the Cork/Moore combination. A few minutes before the ref blew his whistle to end the game, Corky flicked on a Robbie Herrera corner at the near post and Kevin headed home through a crowd of Luton defenders. It was 1-1, but there was still room for injury time drama as Luton piled on the pressure in an attempt to avert the embarrassment of drawing at home to lowly Fulham. I made a good double save from Kerry Dixon, and then another good save near the finish, while Robert Haworth almost intercepted a back pass at the other end which could have given us the winner.

Even though the game finished level, it was an excellent result for us. I was named Man of the Match, something which seldom seemed to happen to players from visiting teams, especially goalkeepers, and I was presented with a Coca-Cola watch – which I still have in a drawer somewhere. It's a very nice, good quality watch and it's probably in the same drawer as the video I have of this game; the trouble is, I can't work out which drawer it is! Our chairman at the time, Jimmy Hill, referred to that timepiece in an interview after the game. He said the ref had seemed to play about 30 minutes overtime, but that he couldn't check it because Jim wasn't yet wearing his new watch.

I have to say that it was very nice to be congratulated by so many people. The travelling Fulham fans were, of course, tremendous, and chairman Hill came up and congratulated me on a fine performance. Even Ian Branfoot seemed pleased with me. And Mr Branfoot did not give praise lightly. One local paper headed its report "Stannard Works Miracles" and awarded me ten out of ten for my performance on the night. I liked that!

I've managed to find a copy of the programme for the second leg, which has a report on the first game. Kevin Moore and I both come in for a lot of praise, and my bits read like this:

As early as the fifth minute, Jim Stannard registered his claim on the Coca-Cola Man of the Match Award, with a superb one-handed save from former Chelsea star Kerry Dixon. Stannard was called into action 20 minutes later, when David Preece tried his luck. As the first half drew to a close, Paul Telfer was the next in line to try his luck but Fulham's number one keeper proved to be master of his goalmouth. The biggest early season shock for Luton must have been Big Jim's determination to send the Black and Whites into the dressing room at half-time without conceding a goal.

In the second half, Jim Stannard continued to stand firm. He was forced into action once again when a Scott Houghton shot went past the post.

It was always going to have to be a sensational goal to beat Stannard, and when it came it certainly fitted that bill. Scott Oakes sent a 25-yard piledriver scorching into his net, giving the keeper no chance at all.

Whoever wrote that can be forgiven for leaving out a few saves. I can't really remember them all properly myself.

We faced Luton again a week later, this time at the Cottage in front of what was, at that time, a fair-sized crowd of over five thousand. Would Jim turn up trumps yet again? It's not for me to say of course, but I'll say it anyway: I had another very good game. We were one up at half-time, with a strike from Robert Haworth, and once more I felt I would keep a clean sheet. Once more I was wrong, as it turned out, but we drew 1-1 again and then won the tie 4-3 on penalties – with yours truly saving the final spot-kick from Dwight Marshall. We had earned ourselves a second round tie against First Division Stoke City. We won the first of these games 3-2 at the Cottage, but then lost 1-0 at Stoke and went out on the away goals rule. That was a shame. I felt we might have gone a bit further that year.

As it happened, 1994-95 was my last season at Fulham. Towards the end of the campaign, I injured the biceps on my right arm in a game at Scarborough (I think it was Scarborough, but it may have been at Scunthorpe – I did play in quite a few games!) It was quite a bad injury and I returned to the side three weeks later with the injury far from healed and played well in a 1-1 draw at Mansfield. The manager congratulated me on my performance, but it turned out to be my last game for Fulham. I had conceded 47 goals in 36 Division Three games, so it was not my best ever season, but it was not all that bad either – and I had kept nine clean sheets.

As I've already suggested, I never wanted to leave Fulham and I was surprised, and frankly quite angry, when Ian Branfoot decided to let me go to Gillingham. I felt I had given the club loyal service and, at 32, which is not old for a goalkeeper, it was a disappointment that I was no longer wanted. Micky Adams took over as player-manager not long afterwards, and I wonder what would have happened had he taken charge of the team a little earlier. Perhaps he would have persuaded Branfoot, who had become general manager, to keep me on. I had been Player of the Season at Fulham on several occasions, and I think my later record at Gillingham suggests that it might have been quite a good idea to keep me at the Cottage for a few more years.

Even though things did not always go well for us, I thoroughly enjoyed my time at Fulham. The fans were marvellous and I always enjoyed the banter. In the book about Fulham goalkeepers, published a few years ago, a supporter called Dylan Mason wrote:

Big Jim was, and still is, widely regarded as one of the best reflex shot stoppers outside the Premiership. His substantial physique, combined with superb agility, made him a cult figure down by the Thames.

I'll buy Dylan a drink if I ever meet him.

I was very disappointed that we didn't win anything while I was at Fulham, especially as I achieved promotions at both Southend and Gillingham. When they return, playing for another team, most footballers say they like to put one over on their old club. I didn't feel like that when I was in the Gills' goal, facing Fulham. Of course, as a professional, I did my best to stop the Cottagers from scoring but, even though I had a great time at Gillingham and established a lot of rapport with the fans there, my heart was always with Fulham. It still is. I always look for their results first – then I look at Gillingham's.

Of course, I'm still in touch with some of my old muckers. Glen Thomas has always been a special mate, and I often meet up with Gary Brazil and Duncan Jupp – who is currently with Southend. I'm still in touch with Fulham too, occasionally appearing on Club Call and I've also been back to the Cottage as Guest of Honour. Mind you, the lady in charge didn't know who I was, and didn't seem to believe I was the Guest of Honour – for some reason (I can't think why) she thought I wasn't a former professional athlete – so I had a bit of trouble actually getting in. Still, I've been told that Pat Nevin couldn't get in for Gerry Peyton's testimonial game against Chelsea – and he was in the team!

When I went back, a few of the fans didn't seem to know who I was either, but I suppose that's bound to happen when a club suddenly has money, and a lot of success, and a load of new supporters quickly make an appearance. Some of them probably hadn't heard of Johnny Haynes! Of course, I did get a wonderful reception from the fans who remembered me – especially those at the Hammersmith End. I'm actually very glad Fulham have finally risen to new heights. It's a big job for a young manager like Chris Coleman. He must have been under a lot of pressure during the last few years, and has done very well indeed. If only that success had come a few years earlier…

When I first went to Fulham, I remember Les Strong saying to me: "Play as long as you can, because you'll be retired for a very long time". I was 17 or 18 at the time, and I didn't take too much notice of these words of wisdom (it's funny how a complete nutcase like Les can come out with words of wisdom!). He was, of course, right, and I wish now that I had been able to go on playing for a bit longer. I was 38 when I stopped playing, not all that old for a 'keeper – look at Dave Beasant – and could actually have gone on for two or three more years had I not received slightly dodgy advice regarding an injury.

I do miss playing, but I'm kept pretty busy all the same. A few years ago the wife and I bought a pub in rural Essex (don't tell Andy Sayer), which had closed its doors to customers for the last time. It needed a lot of work to convert it into a family home, and we've been working on it ever since, but I have to say I'm quite proud of it. I've had quite a few coaching jobs since I retired, and I've currently got three part-time jobs. I've run a coaching school for the last eight years, and that takes up three nights a week. I love doing it, but it doesn't pay much!

I also coach at Leyton Orient, but my main job is that of manager of Redbridge in the Ryman Premier League. I was asked to take over in January 2004, when the team was bottom of the Conference South and really struggling. It was a bit too late to stop the team from being relegated, but I'm naturally hoping to help them bounce back to higher status. Football in the lower leagues is improving, partly I think because, with all the great foreign players being signed by league clubs, we sometimes get the chance to snap up players who might otherwise have gone to clubs at a higher level.

Redbridge used to be known as Ford United – so "Big Jim" has in fact returned to his old club, where it all began. That's fine, but I hope for bigger things in the future and would love to be back at Fulham in some capacity one day. Meanwhile, I'd better get on with the managing, the coaching – and the DIY work.

SIMON MORGAN
DEFENDER 1990–2001

BORN   5th September 1966, Birmingham
SIGNED   12th October 1990 from Leicester City; £100,000
FULHAM CAREER   408 games, 53 goals
HONOURS   1 Second Division Championship, 1 Third Division
promotion, 2 England U21 caps
LEFT   Free transfer to Brighton, June 2001

A rare shining light in a half-decade of mediocrity, Simon Morgan gave a
decade's loyal service as a midfielder and latterly a central defender. His England
Under 21 prospects, bright at Leicester, never translated into full international
honours, but as a clubman he has never been bettered. "Mr Fulham" left in
2001 to join Micky Adams' Brighton, but was already promising to return – and
he did so in 2002 to become the club's Community football supremo.

Aston Villa 0 v Fulham 2

FA Cup Fourth Round
23 January 1999

Villa Park
Attendance 35,260

Two divisions' difference overturned as Fulham win at Villa Park

Teams

Michael Oakes	Maik Taylor
Steve Watson	Steve Finnan
Gareth Barry	Rufus Brevett
Ugo Ehiogu	Simon Morgan
Gareth Southgate	Chris Coleman
Riccardo Scimeca	Kit Symons
Ian Taylor	Steve Hayward
Lee Hendrie	Paul Bracewell
Alan Wright	Geoff Horsfield
(Sub. Darius Vassell)	
Julian Joachim	Paul Peschisolido
	(Sub. Neil Smith)
Paul Merson	Wayne Collins

Scorers   Morgan 8, Hayward 43

Referee: D Elleray

WHEN FULHAM WERE drawn away to Villa in the FA Cup Fourth Round in January 1999 we fancied our chances. Not in an arrogant way, but because we were riding high in the Second Division. Win, lose or draw we were going to give it a right go. This was a very special game for me, but I very nearly missed it. I'd been out injured – I'd had a few injuries around that time, I think it was a groin problem this time – and I'd missed a few weeks. The weekend before, I'd started training again on the Friday while the team went to Manchester City and lost 3-0 on the Saturday.

Manager Kevin Keegan had gone for a different system up there, a flat back four, whereas he had been adopting a five-man defence previously. Then on the Thursday before the Villa game Alan Neilson tore a hamstring; that probably made the decision for Kevin – I was back in with a shout! Having managed a week's training I had a fair idea that I'd be playing, but you never knew what Kevin's team was going to be until 2pm. We had a very low-key training session on the Friday, basically just a few set pieces, and Kevin kept it very muted on the coach up to Villa.

I was eager to play for all sorts of reasons. One was that Villa had chucked me out in my younger days – they didn't think I was good enough. So yes, I was very keen – in fact I'd have been devastated if I'd missed out. The circumstances leading up to the game were all a matter of fate, and then when I turned on the telly on the morning of the match the first thing I saw was "Morgan passed fit to play" on Sky Sports News. Which was good to see! Especially as it was the first I'd heard of it. I had no nerves whatsoever, just a genuine sense of anticipation. As KK had ensured a low-key build-up it really was just like "any other game". We were very confident, and Kevin had fired everyone up from the week before; the training had been very good and geared not so much towards beating Villa, but more a case of getting back to basics and "let's go and show everyone what a good team we are."

Most Fulham fans know my Birmingham connections – I've always been a Bluenose! – and then there was Stevie Hayward who came from the area, too. We probably claimed half the match tickets between us! On the ticket front, I seem to remember that the club took some flak from the Fulham fans – they'd been offered 6,000 tickets from Villa, but decided to take a smaller allocation, around 4,000 I believe, and sold those very easily. There was a clamour for more. The knock-on effect of this was that the players were restricted at first as to how many tickets they could have – so I had to beg, steal and borrow to get 50-odd tickets for my nearest and dearest. In fact the whole lead-up to the game was a series of phone calls from fellow Bluenoses demanding that "you've got to beat those Villa bastards", while a big chunk of my family were actually Villa fans so it all got very involved…

But the funny thing was we barely spoke about Villa during the build up. Their manager, John Gregory, was a very high-profile character and had been spouting off about how fantastic they were, while Kevin was the complete opposite and played the whole game down. In the previous round Kevin had sounded a rallying cry to our fans to turn up for the home replay with Southampton – and they'd turned out in their thousands and many were locked out of the Cottage. This time he played everything down, but such was the way the fans were feeling about things that the Villa tickets went virtually overnight and we took a noisy following up there. The scene was nicely set.

There we were in the away dressing room at Villa Park and Kevin Keegan still hadn't mentioned our illustrious opponents. The teamsheet was posted up, and we saw that star striker Stan Collymore wasn't on it. We didn't know anything about the circumstances – that he simply hadn't turned up – but as a defender, the reaction was "Thank God for that!"

Villa had beaten Everton 3-0 during the week to stay at the top of the Premiership, and that might have done us a favour. We were going to react positively, we had to; we had to bounce back after that defeat, whether we ended up winning, losing or drawing. On the other hand they'd gone joint top, were now playing a team from the Second Division, and were the "big cheese", and thought they were probably in for an easy game. So there were all these factors conspiring – while the Collymore episode must have had a massive impact in their dressing room.

One of those footballing twists meant that Stan was a Fulham player not long after. And of course we gave him no end of stick. We thanked him many, many times for not turning up and told him that his absence was pivotal! He's an odd one, Colly. I think "complex character" is the best way to describe him.

Our five-man defence that season featured Chris "Cookie" Coleman, Kit Symons and yours truly as the middle threesome. It had to be my favourite season for action on the pitch – we got on well and we continually took the mick throughout games. We not only stopped most of what was thrown at us, but managed to weigh in with a fair number of goals, too. People said that we must have worked at it really hard, but Cookie and Kit were quality international players, which made things so easy for me – all I had to do was sweep up behind them! The first time we tried it in pre-season, Kevin wasn't even there – he was away on holiday. Coach Frank Sibley took the training session and it was Frank who persuaded Kevin to stick with the system. Once we started winning 1-0 and 2-0 – it wasn't necessarily pretty that season – it settled down wonderfully for us as we were keeping clean sheets and winning. Sounds easy, doesn't it? In fact it got us promoted with a record number of points.

We had a lot of dependable pros at Fulham then, as well as top men such as Kit and Cookie. You could put Paul Trollope and Wayne Collins in that dependable category. And certainly Rufus Brevett and Geoff Horsfield. Then we had real quality in Steve Finnan. Everyone knew, even at that time, that Finns was exceptional. He had so much time on the ball and was so good in possession. He was a quiet lad who simply got on with things. And now he's a European Cup winner.

Anyway, there I was in the dressing room at Villa, just starting to get changed for the game, when this massive figure came in through the door – it was the last person I wanted to see at that point, a certain Philippe Albert from Newcastle. He was joining Fulham – a lovely fella as it turned out, and one who fitted in right away with the boys – and my position was the one up for grabs. The guys in the dressing room sensed that straight away and were soon rallying around me – we were minutes away from a big match, all said and done – and taking the piss out of the new arrival. It wasn't difficult. He had the dodgiest pair of shoes and a ridiculous suit, plus a plain daft Geordie/Belgian accent!! I tried to laugh it off, but perhaps that, too, added something to the mix. It might even have been good kidology on Kevin's part.

It had been one hell of a transformation for the club in those two to three years as well, don't forget. We'd been down amongst the deadbeats, then, even though we got promotion from the bottom division, the best we could really have hoped for that next season was a mid-table finish. But with the advent of Mohamed Al Fayed came a whole new level of expectation; by the time Kevin Keegan took over the manager's hot seat from Ray Wilkins we were on something of a roll. With Keegan going on to manage England, at first on a part-time basis, not long after the Villa game, it proved to be our only full season with him in charge.

But things had changed in such a short space of time; not many Second Division clubs could afford to buy the likes of Chris Coleman for £2 million. But the type and quality of players being acquired was absolutely vital. Take Cookie; he'd been around the lower divisions with Swansea and he knew the mentality needed to move the club upwards. He treated everyone the same, whether it was Kit Symons or Rod McAree. Kit had just been brought in, while Rod was on his way out – it was a revolving door policy at Fulham in those days. But it was essential that the squad spirit was sound, and Cookie made sure of that with a whole host of antics.

Kevin had the task of trying to manage some players out of the door as we evolved pretty quickly. What we did in the dressing room was to have a 'gold card room' for the new signings and 'the leper colony' for the old squad members. Kevin didn't particularly like it, but that's the footballers' humour coming out. And it was an odd time, with some of the new guys not getting into the team right away, so we had the like of Robbie Herrera, Mark Blake and even myself hanging on. We had good characters in Mark Walton, Rod McAree and Darren Freeman – and Cookie could identify with all of them. He wasn't made captain right away, but he was the main man in the dressing room and made sure we were all in it together.

Personally, I'd gone from being leader of the pack to being a very small fish in a big pool, desperately trying to hang on to the good times and be a part of it all. I was quoted in the papers as saying "I want to go all the way with Kevin Keegan", but it wasn't meant to sound that dodgy, honest! You see, Kevin had promised that he'd take Fulham to the top as part of the chairman's five-year plan and I was simply trying to cling on for as long as possible during the club's rise. The tremendous thing was, the wonderful team spirit that got us promoted from Division Three under Micky Adams never changed. That's a huge testament to all involved. It's crazy really as you had the likes of Cookie and Kit being such dominant characters in the dressing room and yet, looking at how things have developed today, you've never seen two more unlikely people progress into management than that pair. They used to laugh their way through training – which often upset Kevin, and also Peter Beardsley – and didn't seem to take things particularly seriously. But then you knew that come kick-off time they'd switch on and give absolutely everything. Which, of course, they did against Villa.

There was a great atmosphere on the day. Our fans had got there early. It was a very big day for the Fulham fans – the worries of promotion had been put to one side and it was a potentially great day out at a Premiership club. There were balloons and scarves galore and plenty of hopes, but no real expectations. It was only after we got back to the dressing room after the warm-up that Kevin turned up the heat a little, saying: "Come on, we can win this."

He continued: "We're not just here for a good day, we are going to win this. There's gonna be a shock today somewhere in the country – do you want your names to be on the back of the Sunday papers? It could be you." Simple as that. His last words were that we should go out onto the field, go straight to our fans and give them a big clap, get them behind us and then give it our all in the match. We also had to try to make sure that Villa kicked towards the Holte End in the first half – as they preferred to do that in the second period. In those final seconds before kick-off we had to keep reminding ourselves to remind Cookie to choose the right end if we won the toss – "plastic captain", me and Kit called Cookie, as we did all the work! – but he managed to do that right. The teams turned round and off we went.

Once the game started the best way to describe things was "comfortable" – and that's not bad when you're a Second Division team playing away at the Premiership leaders. As a defender, it's a good sign if you're not being pulled out of position early on. If you're not put under pressure you settle into the game very quickly. They had a very quick forward in Julian Joachim, but we countered that by playing very deep. In fact we'd play so deep sometimes we'd be behind Maik Taylor! He'd moan at us if anyone got in a shot, but we'd just say "that's what you're there for!" Let's face it, we weren't the quickest back three around.

At the other end, we won a corner after eight minutes or so and us big guns went up. Every day before a match that season we'd spend a good half-hour with Frank Sibley; Stevie Hayward would knock dozens of balls across and Chris, Kit and me would work on various positionings. (We'd done so the day before and, of course, I missed the lot – couldn't hit a barn door!) People would say that season that "you must have had it so worked out" with all the goals we scored. But it was only literally as you got to the opposition box and saw how you were being marked that you decided what would be done on that occasion. Crucially, Stevie would put the ball into such good areas that you could attack it. Our job was to get across our man and attack the ball.

By the time we loped upfield at Villa Park, Stevie had put the ball down and was ready to take the kick and there was this massive gap towards the near post. I remember saying to the other two "I'm going". And I just ran. Scimeca, who was marking me, was looking around or something, but anyway I managed to get a yard on him. Over the ball came and, it was my turn if you like. There was that much pace on the kick that I didn't get a full head on it and it skimmed off the bald patch and I knew immediately that it was in. The keeper wasn't going to get there and Barry on the line, unless he was going to handball it, wasn't going to stop it either.

Cue celebrations. I remember going to the corner, and Paul Peschisolido dragging me over. It was all going fine until bloody Cookie dived on top and splat, I was flattened into the turf! It was the early goal that we'd badly wanted. I have to say – and I'm going to enjoy saying this – that the Villa fans aren't the most supportive when things aren't going their way, they're very quick to turn. They went very quiet. And it was much the same on the park. Villa didn't have too much to offer. There were a couple of occasions near half-time when Joachim had a run at me. Once I tried to nick a pass back to Maik and Joachim got in, but lacked support to make anything of it. They didn't seem to have that extra spark of energy, which was maybe down to that midweek game. But it suited us to a tee.

We had a lot of experience in midfield with Paul Bracewell and Wayne Collins and we kept the ball for long periods and it seemed all too easy. I even remember laughing and joking with the match referee David Elleray! Strikers Pesch and Geff Horsfield gave Southgate and Ehiogu an afternoon to forget. They absolutely blasted them; Geoff was fantastic – they couldn't cope with his big, physical presence. In fact he won the corner that led to my goal. The uncertainty of their centre-backs spread through the Villa team.

We seemed to be in their half all the time and had a number of chances. Pesch missed a header from about an inch out and then, just before half-time, we got the free kick that deflected in; when something like that happens you know that you're onto a winner. Steve Hayward, of course, was all smiles and very happy to claim the goal. Delighted, in fact…

It was a case of "job done – so far" in the dressing room at half time; we were quiet and feeling in control. No doubt the supporters were thinking "We're going to lose this 3-2, typical Fulham" – you see, I know them of old! We weren't cocky, but we weren't worried either. The only drama came with Cookie. Chris was just having a few last words before we went back onto the pitch and he bent down to do up his laces. As he did so, Stevie Hayward lifted his foot up to stretch himself and booted him in the head! Cookie went straight down and was flat out! Everyone's gone "Oh no, what's happened, what's happened?" Then we've realised it's Cookie's head and, of course, he got up without feeling a thing. No sense, and all that…

We knew they'd come at us a bit more in the second half and, so as not to get done by pace, we played that bit deeper. Accordingly our possession was much more in our own half. But we still weren't troubled unduly. I think they had a header about five minutes from time that Maik tipped over the bar. I got cramp with about 15 minutes left. I told Kit that I couldn't do his running any more and that he'd have to start working. He just gave me one of his looks and said "you old tart!"

After Maik made that save our fans seemed to realise it was our day and they went absolutely potty. When the ref blew up for full time I remember jumping all over Cookie – I totally smothered him. And then did the longest lap of honour in the world. I got hold of Paul Merson's shirt for my lad – Merse was big enough to say "Well done, you deserved it". And that picture on the front of this book is of me saluting my family. It was a great moment.

A brilliant moment for Fulham and for yours truly. And made all the sweeter for being a Birmingham fan. There were a couple of people shouting "Shit on the Villa" and I couldn't help smiling. But then I was doing a lot of smiling at the time. And what a great day for the Fulham fans. Many have told me since that the Villa result was when they realised that the chairman's aspirations of taking Fulham to the top wasn't pie in the sky. It wasn't just a case of winning the Second Division, it was going to go way beyond that. It wouldn't be long before we'd be going back to Villa Park in the same League as them. People still talk of the match as one of the great days on the journey up the divisions, along with Carlisle away and Blackburn away to name just two.

Back in the dressing room afterwards it was fairly quiet, just another day at the office. Kevin came in and said "Well done, but remember you've got Oldham on Tuesday; make sure you behave tonight." And he headed off to meet the press. I did a bit for the radio, but escaped most of the press entourage as I was eager to meet the family. I found out that when I'd scored some had jumped up and celebrated – in the Holte End! They took a bit of gyp and tried to explain it away with a betting slip, saying "It's all right, but I've got him as first goalscorer at 33-1". One or two still had a go, so one of my lot got up and said "It's my brother, all right? My brother!" That just about got him out of it.

And no, I hadn't backed myself to score at those odds, unfortunately. Not that I needed any money that evening. Kevin asked us to behave and stay focused. I focused all right – in a little drinking establishment in Birmingham. I didn't have to buy a single drink all night (they were all doubles! Well, they could have been if I'd wished!). Every Birmingham fan in the city wanted to buy me a drink – it meant that much to them! Let alone Fulham fans. So I was well and truly focused! But I was re-focused enough to score the winner against Oldham the following Tuesday (a poor game but great result that took us back to the top of the Second Division, where we stayed). Unfortunately I pulled a hamstring in that game that went to a nerve in my back, so it was back to the treatment table for the next few weeks.

The cup draw gave us Manchester United away in the fifth round, by which time the Keegan-for-England stuff was big news. I missed the match due to the injury, but we took 8,000 fans to Old Trafford and John Salako missed that sitter that should have earned a depleted side a draw. Kevin's first game as part-time England coach was against Poland. He came into our dressing room before our match against Notts County and asked about our injuries. I told him "It's all right Gaffer, I'll be fine for Poland." He just looked at me and started laughing. Mind you I was one of the few Englishmen at the club at the time! It was a shame that Kevin had said so publicly that he'd stay with Fulham. But then he's such an emotive person. He felt at the time that he hadn't finished at Fulham and he wanted to carry on. But he had to take the England job, no question.

The chairman told us that he'd get another manager and that we'd continue to climb up the divisions and he was true to his word. The club seemed to find the right manager at the right time – so many clubs out there are searching for the right guy…then again, we've had our problems in the past! But Micky Adams, when he took over, was perfect – he had the energy and motivational powers to drag the players, the supporters, the whole club, up by its shoelaces. We failed in the play-offs under Ray Wilkins, but Kevin Keegan pushed things on brilliantly and took us to the Championship. It wasn't particularly exciting under Paul Bracewell, but we established ourselves in the higher division and without that I don't think Tigana could have come and achieved what he did – take Fulham into the Premiership. Tigana revolutionised the club; the fitness levels of the players were unrecognisable, we won our first 11 games and never looked back. I watched most of it from the sidelines having picked up two bad injuries – but he even managed to get me fit again. Just.

Jean was fantastic to me. There was Fulham about to make it into the top flight and he called me into his office. He said: "I think you know as well as I do that there's not a place for you in my Premiership plans – but I want to give you one more game…by the way, what position do you play?" I couldn't help smiling. "You'll be sub against Wolves so that you can say a proper goodbye to the fans." An unbelievable gesture. I went on towards the end of the game – and got a standing ovation for taking a throw-in.

It was the best 12 minutes of my life. Apart from the Villa game, of course!

SEAN DAVIS
MIDFIELD 1996–2004

BORN   20 September 1979, Clapham, London
SIGNED   1 August 1996 as youth player
FULHAM CAREER   186 games, 20 goals
HONOURS   1 First Division Championship, 12 England Under 21 caps
LEFT   Transferred to Tottenham Hotspur, July 2004; undisclosed

Sean broke into the Fulham side which set all sorts of records on its way to winning promotion to the top flight of English football for the first time since 1968 under the guidance of Jean Tigana. A hugely popular and passionate figure, he also scored the goal which clinched the Championship title against Sheffield Wednesday as well as the vital last–gasp winner at Blackburn to defeat Fulham's closest promotion rivals. Now ploughing his furrow at White Hart Lane, when he first started to make himself a name at Craven Cottage then boss Kevin Keegan described him as being "as good as anyone I've seen at his age."

Blackburn Rovers 1 v Fulham 2

Division One
Wednesday 11 April 2001

Ewood Park
Attendance 21,578

Fulham all but mathematically guarantee promotion to the Premiership

Teams

Brad Friedel	Maik Taylor
John Curtis	Steve Finnan
Henning Berg	Rufus Brevett
Craig Short	Andy Melville
(Sub. Eyal Berkovic)	
Keith Gillespie	Kit Symons
(Sub. Craig Hignett)	
David Dunn	Bjarne Goldbaek
Garry Flitcroft	Lee Clark
Alan Mahon	Sean Davis
Damien Duff	John Collins
(Sub. Stig Inge Bjornebye)	
Marcus Bent	Barry Hayles
	(Sub. Alan Neilson)
Matt Jansen	Louis Saha

Jansen 6	**Scorers**	Saha 45, Davis 90
	Sent Off	Brevett 41

Referee: C Wilkes

THE GAFFER USED to hammer me for crossing the halfway line. To this day I still don't know what made me run forward like that. Three minutes into injury time, I suppose the rules kind of go out of the window. But when the ball hit the back of the net in the dying seconds of that game at Ewood Park, it was one of the greatest moments of my life.

With the benefit of perspective, I now realise what an incredible experience the 2000/01 season was. It will live with me forever. No matter what else I go on to do in my career, those ten months can never be bettered. It was one of those rare combinations of time and place – for everybody involved, but for me in particular because it was my baptism, my first taste of regular first-team football. It was a thrilling time that can never be repeated.

Playing in that Fulham side was nothing short of a privilege – the best team and the classiest style of football in which I've ever been involved. Some of the stuff we played, especially when we had our strongest side out, was almost unreal. And the position I occupied – the holding midfield role just in front of the back four – meant I was always involved, simply because we always had the ball.

Looking back on the spine of that side, it's no surprise that we ran the First Division ragged. Maik Taylor in goal is now probably one of the top five or six keepers in the Premiership. Until his accident I had Chris Coleman behind me, Lee Clark just ahead and then Louis Saha leading from the front. That's a strong spine. And when you add in the other players – Barry Hayles, Luis Boa Morte, Steve Finnan and John Collins to name but a few– you can see why we were so much better than anyone else in the League.

The stats tell the story of just how good we were. We shattered records galore – broke the 100-point barrier and equalled the League record for the most wins at the start of a season when we went on that 11-game unbeaten run. Louis Saha scored more goals than anyone in all four divisions with 32 – and when you consider that Boa Morte got 21 and Barry Hayles got 19, that's a lot of goals! Out of our 46 League games that season, we only lost five. That says it all. We were on fire.

For me, it was my breakthrough year, so it will always be special for that reason alone. But to emerge in a team like that – how do you top it? I was only 21. I'd been on the fringes for the previous two or three seasons. The year before, 1999-2000, I felt I was ready to push on. But Paul Bracewell, who was manager at the time, didn't seem to have the confidence to involve me every week. Then Jean Tigana arrived. With Platini, Fernandez and Giresse, he was a quarter of one of the most famous midfields in history, the French "Magic Square". He'd been watching a few games at the end of the previous season, so when he started that summer he had a pretty clear idea of who he wanted to work with. As a midfielder myself, to be recognised by someone with his CV was as big a compliment as you could get. I owe so much to Jean Tigana. He introduced the famous diamond midfield to Fulham straight away and identified the holding role as my best position. And that's where I still play now. He was hard on me, no doubt about that. We had our ups and downs, but he certainly bought out the best and was the making of me as a Premiership player.

He wasn't the only influence, of course. Before him a lot of people had played their part. People like Micky Adams, Alan Cork, Kevin Keegan and Paul Bracewell. John Marshall is someone I owe a lot to – he was my youth team coach. He kept my head straight and calmed me down when I needed it. But Jean was the one who gave me my real break. The others helped build the potential, but Jean unlocked it.

I missed the very first game of that season. I was injured. It was against Crewe on a beautiful summer's day at the Cottage; we won 2-0 and everyone could tell that something special was about to happen. My first game came the following Friday night away at Birmingham. I was back to full fitness and Jean put me straight in the side and, from then on, I was always on the team sheet, providing I was fit. I'll never forget that night as long as I'll live. We absolutely battered them 3-1; I scored the third and after the game we all just sat in the dressing room looking at each other, thinking, "flippin' 'ell!" It was a sign of things to come.

Jean was never one for shouting – he just used to tell us to get out there and play, and with the natural flair and ability we had in the team we didn't need to do much more than that to beat people. If you look at the PFA First Division team for that season, there were six Fulham players selected (me included!) which says it all. A lot of people have since said that we were like a Premiership side playing in the First Division. But I for one had never set foot in the Premiership, nor had quite a few of the others in the side. And once we got into the Premiership, it certainly wasn't a bed of roses. There just seemed to be something in the water in 2000/01. And things just seemed to get better and better as each month passed.

There was a great blend of youth and experience in the side which undoubtedly helped. Some, like Chris Coleman and Kit Symons, have now moved into the coaching side. But some of the younger players have gone on to bigger and better things as players. Steve Finnan is a Champions League winner; Louis Saha plays for Manchester United. That's no coincidence. It was a strong, strong team. I was the real young one in that side, the kid who'd been at Fulham during the dark days. But there I was coming of age in this amazing team that seemed to have the Midas touch.

We were top of the table for virtually the whole season. Watford got up there for a week or two in the first half of the campaign. But we soon reclaimed our rightful place – and then we murdered them 5-0 at the Cottage on Boxing Day! Bolton were also one of the front-runners and ended up coming up with us via the play-offs. We'd shared a 1-1 draw with them at the Cottage in March, just as the run-in was starting. But by the time April came around, it was pretty plain for all to see that it was essentially between us and Blackburn for the title. From the point of view of drama, a rescheduled game at Ewood Park couldn't have come at a better time. We were already about 13 points ahead and we knew if we beat them it would make it more or less impossible for them to catch us.

It was typical of Tigana. Even though we were doing so well, the break in the fixture list for international matches a couple of weeks before that Blackburn game didn't mean any time off. Instead he took the lads over to Marseilles for a 5-a-side tournament! But that was his way, and you'd have to say his methods worked. We got used to the long hours and the double training sessions. We used to moan at the time and days off were very rare. But all the work we did on things like core strength and injury precaution certainly did us good. We were unbelievably fit. And the moaning soon stops when the results start coming in, the points start piling up and you're leaving everyone else in your wake.

The week before Blackburn we'd had a rare goalless draw against West Brom at the Cottage. Not scoring at home was most unlike us, and I had an absolute shocker. West Brom put a man-marker on me and it was one of my worst ever games for Fulham. But it's amazing how quickly things can change in football.

By the time the Blackburn game came round, their manager Graeme Souness was already in full swing, claiming they were far and away the better team. It was pretty outrageous given that we were 13 points ahead of them and had hardly lost a game all season. But by that stage, if anyone was going to pip us to the post of winning the title it was going to be them. They were a strong outfit, no question about that. Souness had good pedigree as a manager, they'd been in the Premiership and won it just six years before. And much like us, they had a side which combined a lot of experience – Flitcroft, Berg, Friedel – with some really promising young players like Damien Duff and David Dunn.

But while Souness' comments were hard to swallow, the fact he rattled a few cages down our way was one of the key ingredients in setting up what was to become our biggest game of the season. It wasn't a play-off. It wasn't even going to decide that we were mathematically up – nothing more than three points was on offer. But everyone knew that if we won we'd be untouchable and that, if Rovers won, they'd still be in the race. We all knew that this was effectively the Championship decider.

In many ways it was a very similar set of circumstances to the Carlisle game in 1997, when Rod McAree famously "put the ball in the Carlisle net" as the song goes. People still talk about it as the game and the goal that got us promoted. I was sitting on the bench that day at Brunton Park – not as a sub, but as 17th man. I was only 17-years-old. That game didn't win us mathematical promotion or anything. But in the same way as Blackburn, it was a clincher. And the scenario was very similar. We were a goal down and then we came back to win with a goal that went down in history. It really was déjà vu!

But there seemed to be much more of a rivalry between us and Blackburn than there ever had been in the run-up to Carlisle four years earlier. The Blackburn game was as much about pride as anything else, and the comments from Souness just inflamed that situation. He's big on the psychological battle, we all know that, and perhaps his comments were as much about winding up his own players as anything else. Who knows what was really behind it? All I know is that it didn't work. We gave everything we had that night and maybe those comments were the difference between us and Blackburn in the end.

Hearing what Jean had to say after the game, and then again after the season had ended, it was obvious that Souness had really got to him. He didn't make a big deal about it at the time, not before the game anyway. Jean would never really speak out of turn about anyone – and, to be honest, he didn't really need to. All the players had heard Souness. We didn't need to tell each other that we had to prove him wrong. We knew it instinctively. It was actually inspiring for us and gave us such a focus. We'd played some incredible football that season. So for Souness to be claiming to be the better side was rich by anybody's standards.

We treated the game very much the same as we'd treat any other. Jean was never one for studying the opposition. It was always about us just playing our own game, and this was no different. The pre-match speech was the same as it ever was: "Play, play…be strong…stay calm." But, it wasn't a normal pre-match dressing room. Everyone could feel that this was a big occasion with a lot riding on it. Don't get me wrong, it wasn't an intimidated feeling. In fact, it was quite the opposite. Everyone was fired up, excited and just itching to get out there. We always were fired up before every game, but this was quite a few notches up from the norm. This was a big, big deal. It was live on Sky and everyone who watches football had their eye on this one.

But there were other reasons too. Chris Coleman's car accident had robbed us of our captain halfway through the season and that really came into play as a huge motivation for everyone. We wanted to win the League for him because he'd been such a big part of Fulham's resurgence. It was so cruel for him to miss out on the very last run to the top, having been such a massive influence all the way along. He'd have loved to have been playing in that game too, especially as it was against his old club. Around that time he'd also had another of what would be numerous operations on his leg, so he was very much in our thoughts. That's why Louis Saha had that T-shirt on under his shirt with 'Cookie We Miss You' scribbled across it – that image has almost become a famous photo in its own right since. People won't know this, but a lot of us had messages for him on T-shirts that night. If ever there was a symbol of solidarity and team spirit that was it. We missed him so much, both on and off the pitch. He was a great player on it, everyone could see that. But he was such a big presence in the dressing room too and you really noticed it when he wasn't there. So we pulled together and everyone wanted it for him as well as for themselves.

Cookie aside, we had a pretty clean bill of health at the time, so we put out a strong side. Maik Taylor was in goal, Rufus Brevett and Steve Finnan were at left and right-back, with Kit Symons and Andy Melville in the middle. Then there was the trademark Tigana diamond midfield with me playing in front of the back four, Lee Clark at the tip of the diamond, Bjarne Goldbaek playing wide right and John Collins on the left. Up front we had Louis Saha and Barry Hayles. And the bench was pretty decent too – we had a World Cup winner on it with Karlheinz Riedle for starters! Then there was Nicolas Sahnoun who could cover my position, Andrejs Stolcers, Alan Neilson and lastly, Marcus Hahnemann as reserve keeper. It was a strong squad. Fabrice Fernandes had been packed off to Rangers by that point, so the only player we were really missing was Boa who must have been injured or suspended.

The atmosphere was electric when we walked out of the Ewood Park tunnel and on to the pitch with 21,500 fans packed in. There was tension in the air, a real sense of occasion. This was a clash of the First Division titans. But almost immediately, we were in trouble. As soon as the game kicked off we were under the cosh. After about five or six minutes, Keith Gillespie broke down the flank and got a cross into the far post which Matt Jansen headed home with ease. We hadn't even got going and we were a goal down. Normally when you go away, you know the home side will come at you to start with, so you try and ride it out for 20 minutes or so until the crowd dies down. But that idea went out the window completely for us. We were on the back foot straight away. Could things get any worse? We didn't know it at the time, but they were about to.

Although it was uphill from the off, we had plenty of confidence in our ability after the season we had put together and we knew that if we kept to our tried and tested passing game we'd create chances, especially with a player like Louis up front. We had a lot of playmakers in the side with the likes of Lee Clark and John Collins and the plan was just to stick to our game and not get flustered. Even when you're away from home, you know that you'll always get a spell when you get possession of the ball and hold on to it for a decent period. We just had to reach that spell. Some people have said we looked nervous to begin with. I don't think we were, and I certainly wasn't. The game was too absorbing for nerves, the tempo certainly higher than usual. Don't forget that we'd been bossing games all through that season. We were used to having all the possession and being in control. This was relatively new territory for us. Blackburn were in the ascendancy and it was a test in the truest sense of the word.

One blessing we did have in that first quarter of an hour was seeing Damien Duff go off injured. He was a hugely influential player for Blackburn and it was one less thing to worry about. But that was the only relief we got – the ref certainly wasn't going out of his way to give us any. When Barry Hayles went clean through on goal, Henning Berg clattered him to the ground in the box. We were convinced it was a penalty, but the ref just waved play on. Minutes later it was poor old Barry again, this time on the end of an elbow in the face from David Dunn. He was cut and bleeding, but the ref managed to ignore that one too. To be honest the standard of referees in the First Division was quite poor overall, so most of the time things like that didn't come as a surprise. As I said, Tigana didn't badmouth anybody much, but he did like a moan about refs! But this was such a big game we just couldn't let things like that get to us. Although they did, as we were soon to discover.

It was just before half-time and the tackles were flying in. Garry Flitcroft and Rufus went for a ball and Rufus seemed to be wrestled to the ground. He was always a fiery player on the pitch – a pansy off it, mind you – and didn't take kindly to Flitcroft's approach, especially after what had happened with Barry. In the heat of the moment Rufus flicked his foot out in retaliation – it wasn't even a kick. But the next thing we know, the ref has his red card out and Rufus was off. Jean was always telling us to not get involved with the opposition if they tried to provoke us and not to argue with the ref. But this was a classic symptom of the kind of tetchy game it was. There was a lot of tension and a few bad decisions had been made. And we were a goal down and a man down. At this stage it looked as if Souness' words might prove true.

The player I felt most sorry for in all of this was Barry. He'd given everything in that game. He'd been kicked all over the shop for the cause, and then he got subbed. But under those circumstances we had no option but to reorganise. So we went to two banks of four with just Louis Saha playing up front. And that meant Barry coming off so that Alan Neilson could come on to play left-back. Al had been suffering with calf injuries, so he'd hardly played all season, but he was good to have on the bench just because he could provide cover for a lot of positions – and he'd played at the top level for Newcastle, so you knew you could trust him.

Ironically enough, even though we were a goal down, a man down and we hadn't even reached half time, nobody was panicking. If anything, Rufus getting sent off gave us the kick up the backside that we needed. And about three minutes later the ball was in the back of the Blackburn net. The way things were going I was convinced the ref was going to give a foul against me. Finns had swung in a deep, looping cross from the right into the Rovers box. I don't really know what I was doing up there – I wasn't really meant to leave my own half! As the ball came across I turned my back on Friedel, the Blackburn keeper. As I did, he came over the top of me and dropped the ball and there was Louis, lurking. He just calmly side-footed it in for what was probably his 300th goal that season! As Louis' goals go, it wasn't one of his most spectacular. He normally beats about four players and smashes it into the back of the net. Spectacular it may not have been; but it was the vital lifeline we so desperately needed – and it couldn't have come at a more critical time.

It was a huge relief to be going into that dressing room at half-time knowing we were back on level terms. Everyone was fuming to begin with, just because of the way things had gone against us. But once we got in there and got the door shut, everyone calmed down. The Gaffer was much more animated than usual, urging us to get stuck in, which was not really his style. To be honest, we knew what we had to do in the second half. None of us wanted to lose this one before the game. But after what had happened in the first half, that sense of determination was stronger than ever. Under the circumstances, a lot of teams would have gone out in the second half and tried to play for a draw. But no-one in that Fulham side was going to opt for that. We knew we'd have to work hard, look out for each other and be mindful of the ref. But we weren't leaving without those three points, simple as that.

We managed to keep the ball quite well at the start of the second half. We didn't create many chances, but we certainly defended well and really limited Blackburn's opportunities. There were a lot of leaders in the team, and that played a huge part. Kit Symons was marshalling the defence with complete composure – he won Man of the Match in the end, and rightly so. Melv in particular was shouting and screaming at me as he always did. It used to do my head in, but it was a big help in hindsight. Clarky too – we had a lot of characters who were constantly talking, encouraging, pulling people here, pushing people there.

It was tough going, though. The extra running we had to do to make up for being a man down was a killer. In the last ten minutes they had a couple of very good chances to kill the game off. Jansen had a shot which hit the post, and then Flitcroft, completely unmarked, received the ball on the edge of the box but stuck it over the bar. In hindsight maybe the writing was on the wall for Blackburn by then – when you have chances like that and don't take them, it tells its own story.

The last five minutes were all a bit of a blur. I remember being over in the left back area. God knows why. I had the ball and got it cleared. Then I suddenly came down with the most awful cramp in my calf. I was down for ages in agony. But almost as soon as I was up, we got this break out of nowhere. With Blackburn pushing up looking for the winner all through the second half, we were relying heavily on the counter-attack and somehow the ball fell to Bjarne on the right who broke into their half. They had hardly any players back, so I just ran as fast as my exhausted legs could carry me into the space that had opened up in front of us. Clarky was up there too and heading over towards the left of the box so I just tried to stay in the middle. Bjarne swung the ball over to Clarky who fired off a shot which deflected off a defender – Berg, I think – and seemed to fall into my path. At the time I thought I was offside, but when I've watched it back since I think it's fair to say I timed my move perfectly!

Because of the deflection the keeper was out of the equation, floored, but the ball was spinning all over the place, and as it came to me I just shot. It wasn't an easy one, I can tell you that. But I somehow managed to get my foot over it – it was more instinct than anything else. If I'd have stopped and thought about it, maybe it would have been a different story, and if I got the same chance now I'd probably shank it somewhere!

As the ball left my foot it seemed to move in slow motion towards the open Blackburn goal. And then it crossed the line. That magical moment was quite genuinely one of the greatest feelings I have ever experienced, only beaten since by the birth of my daughter.

After that, all hell broke loose! The whole of the bench came running down the touchline – even Jean! For a man who very rarely celebrated anything, I think that showed just how much it went to him. He looked like Barry Fry – but much skinnier and a different colour, of course! It was at that point that Jean and I hugged each other. That wasn't normal behaviour for me and him which made it seem even more poignant.

And then came my infamous celebration dance. I still get stick for that now! I don't quite know what prompted me to do it – I hadn't rehearsed it or anything. It was completely spontaneous. At the time everyone was listening to garage so it was based on that I suppose. But I've never really lived it down! At least people still remember it!

After that I was absolutely drained. We knew we'd won the game – and the title too. But all the work, effort and emotion of that match hit me at once – I was absolutely dead on my feet, my limbs like lead.

Afterwards, the dressing room was buzzing, even though we were all wrecked. As the coach pulled out of the ground, all the Fulham fans were waiting for us and going absolutely mad. We had Huddersfield away on the Saturday, so we were staying up north instead of coming back to London. It wasn't a really long journey, but, as ever with Jean, there were no celebratory beers on the coach. We could have won the FA Cup and we still wouldn't have been allowed a drink! I was absolutely exhausted, physically and emotionally, when I finally climbed into bed at the hotel that night. But I still couldn't sleep – I often struggle to doze off after games for some reason, but after that one I had absolutely no chance.

The Huddersfield game was a real anti-climax. Even though it was the game where we mathematically secured promotion to the Premiership it just didn't have the sense of occasion that Blackburn had mustered. Jean actually rested me that day – I only came on in the last ten minutes. At the final whistle we celebrated with the "We're Going Up" flags and all the bottles of bubbly. But to be honest, I think that was the emotion from the Blackburn game still running through our veins.

And then came Sheffield Wednesday at home on the following Monday, Easter Bank Holiday. We only needed a point to win the Championship. The Gaffer played American Marcus Hahnemann, who managed to concede a very strange goal on one of his rare first-team outings. I remember Cookie afterwards going on about what the match stats would say – "Sheffield Wednesday shots, zero. Fulham goals conceded, one!" The crowd seemed really subdued at that game. We couldn't believe it on the pitch. We'd just got promoted to the top flight for the first time in 30-odd years and yet the crowd were behaving as if we were going down!

And then it happened again, the icing on the cake of the most momentous few days. It was injury time and we were still a goal down. Barry was hobbling – he'd been off the pitch getting treatment on the sideline. We just needed the equaliser and the title was ours and we were running out of time. The Gaffer virtually pushed Barry back on to the pitch. He managed to get the ball to me and I can't really remember anything after that, other than seeing the ball leave my foot and fly into the back net. That was it! We'd equalised in the dying seconds of injury time. I went crazy again, shirt off, pelting down the touchline. At the end of the day it might have only been a point. But it was the point that won us the Championship.

For a defensive midfielder I scored a lot of goals that year, and the one at Blackburn, important and difficult as it had been, wasn't my most spectacular. If I was to pick my favourite, I'd have to say the Sheffield Wednesday one pips it to the post. Either that or the one I got against Preston in the December – a long-ranger that went in off the bar. Looking back, I don't think I can ever have a time like that again. To be 21-years-old, to be playing a key part in a team that's getting talked about all over the country in my first proper season – it just can't be repeated. It's certainly the highlight of my career so far and I'm sure you'd find that most of the players in the Fulham side of 2000/01 would say the same.

And, as games go, Blackburn is the one that really stands out. It was a defining moment that's gone down in Fulham folklore. It was just a remarkable night, at the start of a remarkable week in what was the most incredible football season for all of us involved. When it finished, Jean said that his two highlights of that whole campaign had been the 11-game unbeaten run at the start, and the win up at Blackburn. Considering how many highlights there had been that year, it speaks volumes about the huge significance of that night at Ewood Park.

I don't think I'll ever have a week like that in football again. It was like a real-life fairytale. If I could go back in time to that season I'd do it in a heartbeat.

I still watch the Championship video sometimes. It's good to watch when I'm injured and feeling down. But I always end up fast-forwarding it to April. Like all good stories, we saved the best 'til last!

LEE CLARK
MIDFIELD 1999–2005

BORN   27th October 1972, Wallsend
SIGNED   July 1999 from Sunderland, £3 million
FULHAM CAREER   149 games, 20 goals
HONOURS   1 First Division Championship, 11 England U-21 caps,
plus England Schoolboys and England Youth international caps
LEFT   Free transfer to Newcastle, June 2005

Signed by former Newcastle and Sunderland team-mate Paul Bracewell during
his brief spell as manager, after a stuttering start, Lee Clark provided drive and
goals from midfield, in 1999/2000 he finished as the club's leading scorer. Lee
survived various managerial changes to serve under Tigana and Coleman, the
latter making him captain in his own stead. Lee worked tirelessly and led by
example until injury decimated his 2004-05 season and he was controversially
not offered a new contract. He was welcomed back into his home-town club
set-up with a coaching career in mind.

Manchester United 1 v Fulham 3

FA Premier League
Saturday 25 October 2003

Old Trafford
Attendance 67,727

Fulham win at the Theatre of Dreams for the first time since 1963

Teams

Tim Howard	Edwin Van der Sar
Gary Neville	Moritz Volz
John O'Shea	Jerome Bonnissel
	(Sub. Martin Djetou)
Rio Ferdinand	Alain Goma
Mikael Silvestre	Zat Knight
(Sub. Quinton Fortune)	
Eric Djemba-Djemba	Mark Pembridge
(Sub. David Bellion)	(Sub. Junichi Inamoto)
Cristiano Ronaldo	Steed Malbranque
(Sub. Paul Scholes)	
Nicky Butt	Lee Clark
Ryan Giggs	Sylvain Legwinski
Ruud Van Nistelrooy	Louis Saha
Diego Forlan	Luis Boa Morte
	(Sub. Barry Hayles)

Forlan 45	**Scorers**	Clark 3, Malbranque 66
		Inamoto 79

Referee: M Riley

Beating the mighty Manchester United at Old Trafford is not something that many teams get to do. But to captain the side and get your name on the scoresheet, well, how many players can say they've done that?

The events of Saturday 25th October 2003 summed up the entire 2003-04 season for me. We'd been written off and condemned to the drop by just about everyone before a ball had even been kicked. But by May we'd finished in Fulham's highest ever League placing. To captain the side to that record finish was a great honour. I had some good times at Fulham, but that season as a whole and that game at Old Trafford in particular, were my greatest achievements.

It all started in the April of the season before. We were staring down the barrel of relegation when manager Jean Tigana parted company with the club. With five games to go, it was a bold move – especially as the temporary replacement was a 34-year-old with no managerial experience to speak of. But Chris Coleman had been a great leader on the pitch as captain – and, if it hadn't been for the car accident that so cruelly robbed him of his career, he still would have been wearing the armband. He certainly had a presence around the place and all the players respected him. We knew something had to change – and quickly – and all welcomed the idea, me in particular.

I'd had a lot of trouble with a calf injury that season. I'd been out for ten months in all, but by that stage I'd managed to get fit again. Yet Tigana still didn't seem too keen on playing me. Since we'd made it into the Premiership, I'd spent so much time in the treatment room and, in the meantime, Jean had signed a lot of other midfielders. Perhaps he was just showing some faith in them given the money he'd spent, but it wasn't doing me any good. I just couldn't get into his team. And if I did, it was only ever one appearance before I was back out again. When you've been out for almost a year, the one thing you need above all is a decent run of games. It was a vicious circle.

Tigana left on the Thursday [17th April 2003]. We had a massive game against Newcastle at our temporary home of Loftus Road on the Saturday. With five games remaining, we needed at least two wins to be sure of staying up – and, for a club in Fulham's position, the ramifications of relegation just didn't bear thinking about. We'd been on a complete downward spiral. It's a dangerous position when you find yourself looking at the games coming up and wondering where the next win will come from. We'd just been spanked 3-0 by Man United, 4-0 by Blackburn at home and then 2-0 at Liverpool. Chris had a massive job to do; we all did. He knew that something had to change and fast. Immediately he made a radical switch from a 4-4-2 to a 4-5-1 system. More importantly for me, I was back in the side.

Being against my home-town club Newcastle, my first game back couldn't have been scripted any better – and I scored the winner too as we nicked it 2-1. We went on to get three wins and a draw out of those last five games, more than enough to secure another season of Premiership football, and enough for Chris to be offered the job on a permanent basis.

Any player will tell you that how a team finishes its season has a direct bearing on the mood in the pre-season that follows. That was never truer than in this case. After the thrilling end to the season, everyone was buzzing when they reported back at the end of June. For me in particular, I couldn't wait for the new campaign to start. I'd missed so much football and was itching to be playing again, and under Chris I knew I would be. I didn't really take any time off that summer. I kept coming into the Fulham training ground at Motspur Park while the other lads were away just so I could work on my fitness ahead of the pre-season schedule. I'd missed so much time through injury that I wanted to make sure I got the absolute maximum out of pre-season and didn't want to be playing catch-up.

Even though Fulham had been in the Premiership for two seasons already, it was almost the start of my personal Premiership career with Fulham. I know I'd played for Fulham in the top flight but, with the injuries I'd had, I'd never really had the opportunity to get going since we'd come up. I'd never built up any rhythm. But there I was back in the side. I knew I'd pretty much always be on the team sheet, provided I was fit and playing to the best of my ability. And that was a great feeling after all I'd been though.

Despite the mood of optimism at Motspur Park, it seemed that everyone else on the planet, and the media world in particular, were writing us off as dead certs for relegation. It was *The Sun,* if I remember rightly, who had 11 out of their 12 football writers picking us for the drop. But that didn't bother us at all. We knew that if we got our heads down and followed the instructions of the coaching staff, we had every chance to prove people wrong. We knew we had the players – with Malbranque, Boa Morte and Saha we had no shortage of match-winners in the team. But we also knew, above all else, that we would have to work as hard as we possibly could in every single game to stand a chance. We had to tell ourselves that we weren't one of the top teams in the League, that we wouldn't have the luxury of just turning up, not playing well and still picking up results. We knew we would have to earn every single point, and that meant almost treating every game as if it was our last. If we didn't, we'd be in trouble.

To be honest the lads didn't even talk about what people were saying outside of Motspur Park. We just knew that if we did things right and applied ourselves in the right way we'd surprise a few people. It's not a bad position to be in, when everyone's writing you off. It's almost better than when people have unrealistic expectations. But I don't think even we felt we'd have a season like we did.

The campaign kicked off against Middlesbrough at Loftus Road, and this was a game that really set the tone for how things would go. Both sides played really well, but we came out of the traps absolutely flying that day. By full-time we'd scored three goals, Edwin had saved a penalty and we had our first three points on the board. What a contrast to the season before, but unfortunately a contrast to the following Saturday too. Our first away game was at Goodison Park. After the tail end of the Tigana era, a lot of emphasis was placed on improving our away form because we'd been too much of a soft touch on the road. So we went up to Everton brimming with confidence – and got thumped 3-1!

After the Boro performance perhaps we thought we only had to turn up and it would come. In hindsight it was the kick up the backside, the wake-up call we needed. It reaffirmed that we'd have to fight tooth and nail for every point we wanted to win. If we'd have played badly and still nicked a result we wouldn't have got that call and maybe the next matches would have entirely different outcomes, especially the following week at Spurs.

It was after our trip to White Hart Lane that people started to take us seriously. Beating Tottenham 3-0 on their own patch was something that couldn't be ignored. And from there, we kicked on to put in a string of great away performances, beating Blackburn at Ewood Park, and drawing with ten men in a real battle at St Andrews. We were flying at home, too. We thought we'd done enough to beat Man City until Anelka popped up in injury time to equalise, but it was a great Fulham performance nonetheless and that was what mattered. We were playing with real conviction. It was the kind of football people had previously said we weren't capable of producing. But we were proving to everyone that we could.

As October dawned, it only took a couple of wobbly results for the doubters to come out again. A 0-0 home draw with newly-promoted Wolves was followed in midweek by the visit of Newcastle to Loftus Road. We came out of the traps at quite a pace and within about a quarter of an hour were 2-0 up. I'd put us ahead after three minutes and then Louis Saha got a second not long after. We were flying, we had them under the cosh – it couldn't have been a better start. But somehow we allowed them to muscle their way back into the game and, thanks to Mr Shearer, we ended up losing 3-2. It was one of the best performances by a striker you're ever likely to come up against.

When you've been 2-0 up at home, ended up losing 3-2 and your next fixture's an away trip to Old Trafford it can lead to a few nerves. The midweek Newcastle game hadn't left us a whole lot of time to focus on United. But on the Friday we did the usual and spent a fair bit of time talking about their strengths and how we could stop them from playing. Nine times out of ten when you play United at Old Trafford, they'll end up having the majority of the ball and we knew that stopping that was going to be a key factor. What we didn't anticipate is that it would be United trying to stop us.

United had beaten Rangers in the Champions League during the week, and a win against us would have sent them back to the top of the Premiership so we knew we were going to be in for a tough afternoon. But despite that, and despite what had happened in the week against Newcastle, I was really looking forward to the game – we all were. Going to somewhere like Old Trafford is what being in the Premiership is all about. That's the beauty of the top flight – you bounce from one fantastic fixture to the next. As a venue, Old Trafford really is one of the all-time cathedrals of football. It's certainly the best stadium in the Premier League to visit as an away team. When you step out on to that pitch it's just got this incredible aura about it. You can feel that history has been made there. It's not daunting though. If anything, it's the opposite – you're buzzing at the prospect of playing there. It's why you want to be a footballer for in the first place.

We knew it was going to be an unbelievably hard game but, at the same time, we knew we had an opportunity to get a positive result. I remember being in the dressing room beforehand when we found out that Alex Ferguson had changed the team and left out Roy Keane from the 16 entirely and Paul Scholes was only on the bench. I mean, when it's Manchester United you're talking about, you know full well that whoever gets brought in will still be a top-class player. You don't get even near that squad unless you're up there with the very best. But we knew that leaving out two such influential names would give us an opportunity, provided we did things right, and the news certainly gave us a boost.

Once we got out there and started playing, everything seemed to fall into place almost immediately. Everything we'd wanted to achieve at the start of the season – the way we wanted to play, with and without the ball – seemed to knit together perfectly at Old Trafford that afternoon.

The game couldn't have got off to a better start – mind you, I'd said that about Newcastle! I'd scored after six minutes in that one, but managed to stick one away after three this time. Steed Malbranque dispossessed one of the United defenders – Silvestre, I think it was – and played it into the near post. I just managed to get the side of my foot on to it and glance it past Tim Howard. I think my goal celebration was slightly more animated than it had been against Newcastle during the week – everyone knows that I don't like to celebrate scoring against Newcastle out of respect for the fans. But I was quite happy to celebrate at Old Trafford!

If I'm honest, when that early goal went in I couldn't help but think back to the Wednesday night when we'd got two in the first 12 minutes and then went on to lose. There was an element of "here we go again – are we going to drop off like last time?" But in retrospect I think we'd learned our lesson and, if anything, that goal gave us the confidence to really take the game to United.

It was one of those days when everything ran like clockwork. We seemed to have a lot of space in midfield, we were keeping the ball well, and almost everything we tried to do seemed to come off. We were having bags of possession, the movement was great, we were spraying it about, moving at the right time, playing one and two touch, and getting the likes of Boa and Steed on the ball in the right areas. That was always going to be a key factor as we knew they would be the ones to cause them problems in the final third.

Louis Saha was being a real handful in the United defence too – they were really struggling to cope with him. He was on fire that season, playing in the lone striker role. Not many players could pull that off in the way he did. He didn't grab the headlines that day by scoring himself, but he didn't do himself any harm in the eyes of Alex Ferguson, who signed him a couple of months later. It was certainly no surprise when they came looking for him in the January transfer window.

Ferguson was watching from the stands that afternoon as he was part-way through serving a touchline ban. Whether it had an effect on proceedings, I don't know. You'd have to ask the United players that. But I'm sure he's a forceful presence on the bench. If he'd been standing on the touchline while we'd been bossing the game in the way that we were, well, we all know about the infamous Fergie hairdryer! Perhaps if a couple of the United players had found themselves on the end of that it might have kicked them on a bit. But we were playing so well and with so much confidence, I don't even think that would have made too much of a difference.

In the last minute of the half, Forlan popped up with an equaliser for United. It wasn't down to any particular mistake on our part – it was just one of those things. The whistle went pretty much straight after, and I was very keen to get everyone in the dressing room to regroup as soon as we could. As captain, I knew it was my responsibility not to let the lads get too downhearted because United had scored. Things like that can really knock the stuffing out of you after you've been playing so well, and the one thing we had to keep ourselves from doing was panicking just because they'd equalised. We just had to get it into our minds to keep doing what we had been.

It had been a brave performance so far, we weren't losing and there really wasn't anything for us to get downhearted about. We always knew they'd get chances. Okay, so they put one away just before half-time. But it was crucial that we carried on as we were. After the first-half performance we had every reason to believe that we could take something from the game and it was essential that we retained that positive attitude.

Once the second half got under way, I felt pretty comfortable that we hadn't been flustered by their equaliser. We were still playing with the courage and conviction that had characterised the first 45 minutes. Just after the hour mark I found myself in an ocean of space in the middle of their half and played a long ball over to Boa on the left. Boa played it into Louis Saha who, as ever, was lurking on the edge of the box. Louis knocked it down for Steed Malbranque, who just belted it first time into the back of the net. Once again we'd taken the lead against the Champions, and what a well-worked all-round team goal it was. That summed up the way we'd been playing all afternoon. The confidence, the way everyone was picking the right pass at the right time. On certain days, things just happen for a team, and when it does everything feels effortless.

At 2-1 we still had nearly half an hour left on the clock, and at a place like Old Trafford you'd be naïve to think that the game was over by that point. Then they brought Scholes on for Ronaldo, a pretty clear indication that they were still chasing the game. For us it was a case of, "do we carry on the way we are or do we sit back and try and soak up their pressure?" But if you start doing that against United, you're asking for trouble. The only way was to carry on the way we were. The more the clock ticked, the more they came at us. But in many ways that played into our hands. For the last 20 minutes or so we were catching them on the break all the time. I remember Steed having a great chance to score his second and our third. He was one-on-one with Howard, but his first touch just let him down.

As the last quarter of an hour approached, we seemed to be losing a bit of our rhythm and momentum for the first time all afternoon. Maybe it was a bit of tiredness creeping in, maybe it was the fact that United were putting us under a lot of pressure, maybe a bit of both. I remember having the ball over by the left-hand touchline, about 20-25 yards out. Steed, Boa and I were all there just knocking it about between us – short passes, almost at a walking pace, just so we could keep hold of the ball. All of a sudden Steed picked out this amazing ball which looped into the United box. Inamoto must have anticipated where the pass was going because he made what can only be described as a visionary run towards the penalty spot. At full stretch and under pressure from his marker he got on to the end of the pass and touched it into the back of the net. It was just sublime. Ina was technically a very, very good player, often better than people gave him credit for. Perhaps the physical side of the English game was something he'd initially found hard to adjust to, but he was getting to grips with it by then. But if evidence was needed to show his abundance of talent, that goal was it.

If I was to be objective about the goals we scored that day, I'd have to say that third was the best – even though I scored the first! The way we kept the ball, slowed the game down and then just hit them quickly with a great ball, combined with the run and finish, was stunning.

When that final whistle went, it was one of those magical moments that you want to bottle. To come off the pitch at the end of 90 minutes knowing you've just beaten the Champions 3-1 at Old Trafford is some feeling. And the best thing about it from our point of view is that it wasn't a fluke. We hadn't been battered and got a lucky winner. We'd thoroughly deserved those points and the fact that we got applause from what must have been pretty disgruntled United crowd says it all. Even Ferguson himself admitted afterwards that it was a fully deserved victory – and you don't hear him saying that very often.

You have to give the Fulham management team some credit. Their tactics worked perfectly. But the players implemented them perfectly too. And it wasn't like we just caught United on the counter, either. If you look at the number of chances we had, it shows how much we really took the game to them. We didn't have a bad player on pitch that day. We didn't carry one individual – there were no passengers.

As you can imagine, the dressing room was a pretty happy place to be afterwards and the lads were absolutely buzzing. We knew it would go down as one of the results of the season, but at the time it didn't really occur to us that it would also go down as a massive result in the club's history. It's only later that you see it from that perspective.

I didn't actually travel back with the team that night. One of my horses was running at Aintree on the Sunday so I stayed up in the North West. I don't know what the atmosphere was like on the bus home for the lads – although I can imagine! All I know is that I had a great day at the races. I can't remember if my horse won or not, but to be honest, I wasn't really that bothered after what had happened the day before!

That game, to my mind, epitomises everything that season stood for. The team spirit, the quality we always knew we had, the togetherness in the face of potential adversity. They were qualities which we displayed throughout 2003-04.

We finished ninth that year, a club record position. But there is no question that the results in the first half of the campaign made that possible. We all took a huge boost from such a positive start and it gave us the platform we needed. We were in fourth in the League for a good few weeks before Christmas which surpassed even our own expectations. One minute we'd been certainties for the drop, and the next thing we know people are talking about Europe. Just goes to show how fickle the football world can be.

In hindsight, we had a good balance in the side that year. Sylvain Legwinski, "Leggy", was the holding midfielder whose job it was to try and win the ball. We had Steed with his trickery, Boa's speed, Louis's finishing up front. We had two new full-backs in Moritz Volz and Jerome Bonnissel who were doing really well in their first season in the Premiership, and obviously Edwin Van der Sar in goal. It was a good squad of players and 4-5-1 really suited us.

It was a relatively unused formation in the top flight at that time. Chris was a big fan, having played that way with Wales under Mark Hughes, but that year we really seemed to have the personnel to really pull it off. It's been adopted by more teams since, and it's also been criticised as being negative when things don't go so well. But for us that season, when it worked it was anything but negative.

That game and that season are up there at the top for me in terms of my best times at Fulham. I'd even say it pips the First Division title-winning season to the post. To take a club to its highest ever finish in its history when you're up against some of the best teams and the best players in the world is a great achievement and one of which I'm still very proud.

Not many teams can say they went to Old Trafford, played the Champions off the park and won by two clear goals. The teams that win up there are the ones that play without any fear, and who take the game to United. Okay, you hope for a bit of luck and that you'll catch United on an off day, and maybe United weren't firing on all cylinders that afternoon. But any game involves two teams, and on the day we were brilliant too. You don't beat United by two goals and say it was a fluke. They didn't play well because we didn't allow them to. We didn't let them dictate the game to us, we dictated it to them, and the performance epitomised everything we were about that season. The spirit, passion, work ethic – they were all part and parcel of what Fulham Football Club was about at the time. And for me personally, to have been captain and to have got on the scoresheet as well, it doesn't get much better than that.

I was involved in some great games at Fulham. But Manchester United at Old Trafford in October 2003 will always live in my memory as the greatest game in my Fulham career.

Subscribers

Baker, Philip	Spurs 3-2	League 2003
Beasley, Martin & Dennis	Spurs 3-1	League Cup 1999
Bliss, Tony	Spurs 3-0	League 2004
Brewer, Jonathan	Man Utd 3-1	League 2003
Brooks, Michael John	Northampton 4-2	League 1966
Brooks, Ray	Everton 2-1	FA Cup 1975
Browning, J	Ipswich 10-1	League 1963
Cain, Bob	Maidstone 6-2	AWS 1991
Carter, John	Norwich 6-0	League 2005
Chaston, Martin		
Chaston, Pamela	Sheff W 6-2	League 1958/9
Conroy, Ray	Birmingham 1-0	FA Cup semi-final replay 1975
Dann, Tony		
Dyball, Robert	Aston Villa 2-0	FA Cup 1999
Elliott, David	Northampton 4-2	League 1966
Evans, John C	Blackburn 2-1	League 2001
Evans, Matthew	Aston Villa 2-0	FA Cup 1999
Evans, Simon	Carlisle 2-1	League 1997
Facer, J	Birmingham 1-0	FA Cup semi-final replay 1975
Fanthom, Bernard	Man Utd 3-1	League 2003
Fennell, Robert	Ipswich 10-1	League 1963
Finn, Chris	Ipswich 10-1	League 1963
Goldthorpe, James	Blackburn 2-1	League 2001
Goldthorpe, Martin	Birmingham 1-0	FA Cup semi-final replay 1975
Heatley, Drew	Spurs 3-2	League 2003
Heyman, Billy	Blackburn 2-1	League 2001
Hicks, Derek	Lincoln 1-1	League 1982
The Hills Family	Birmingham 1-0	FA Cup semi-final replay 1975
Holford, Ed (LBNo11)	Birmingham 1-1	FA Cup semi-final 1975
Kilpatrick, Iain	Birmingham 1-0	FA Cup semi-final replay 1975
King, David		
Larkins, Basil	Northampton 4-2	League 1966
Leven, Steve	Bologna 2-2	Intertoto Cup 2002
Lloyd, David	Carlisle 2-1	League 1997
Lowings, Peter	Everton 2-1	FA Cup 1975

Lownsbrough, Mike	Aston Villa 2-0	FA Cup 1999
McCrann, Jim	Lincoln 1-1	League 1982
McLaughlin, G	Spurs 3-2	League 2003
McNeela, PA	Sheff W 6-2	1958/9
Pearce Snr, Capt David	Thames Assoc 8-0	League 1932
Priest, Bryan	Birmingham 4-3	League 1979
Prior, Barbara	Norwich 6-0	League 2005
Reisbach, Stephen	Blackburn 2-1	League 2001
Robinson, Herbert	Lincoln 1-1	League 1982
Smith, Ruth	Man Utd 3-1	League 2003
Trieb, Geoffrey	Birmingham 1-0	FA Cup semi-final replay 1975
Waghorn, Mark	Blackburn 2-1	League 2001
Weight, Craig	Norwich 6-0	League 2005
Weight, Graham	Newcastle 4-1	League 2005
Wiggs, John	Birmingham 1-0	FA Cup semi-final replay 1975
Wilson, Dave	Lincoln 1-1	League 1982
Worley, John	Sunderland 2-0	League 2001

Top Games Voted For

Birmingham 1-0	FA Cup semi-final replay 1975	7 votes
Blackburn 2-1	League 2001	5 votes
Lincoln 1-1	League 1982	4 votes
Ipswich 10-1	League 1963	3 votes
Man Utd 3-1	League 2003	3 votes
Northampton 4-2	League 1966	3 votes
Norwich 6-0	League 2005	3 votes
Spurs 3-2	League 2003	3 votes